Company-wide Agility with Beyond Budgeting, Open Space & Sociocracy

Survive & Thrive on Disruption

Jutta Eckstein and John Buck

Company-wide Agility with Beyond Budgeting, Open Space & Sociocracy
Survive & Thrive on Disruption

Jutta Eckstein and John Buck

ISBN 978-1-544672-87-8

Cover design and chapter illustrations: Katja Gloggengießer, www.grellgelb.de

Tweet This Book!

Please help Jutta Eckstein and John Buck by spreading the word about this book on Twitter!

The suggested hashtag for this book is #agilebossanova.

Find out what other people are saying about the book by clicking on this link to search for this hashtag on Twitter:

#agilebossanova

Contents

Acknowledgments

We want to thank our early reviewers, who were courageous enough to look at a premature version of our chapters (in alphabetical order): Eric Abelen, Bjarte Bogsnes, Andrew Buck, Gerard Endenburg, Hendrik Esser, Marc Evers, Aimee Groth, Azy Groth, Michael Herman, Diana Larsen, Evan Leybourn, Yves Lin, Sandy Mamoli, Steve Morlidge, Christa Preisendanz, Annewiek Reijmer. We are really thankful for all these great and serious comments. We incorporated many of them.

Thanks to all of you, sharing your experiences in an insights box: Eric Abelen, Bjarte Bogsnes, Hendrik Esser, Michael Herman, Jez Humble, Anders Ivarsson, Todd Kromann, Tracy Kunkler, Diana Larsen, Yves Lin, Sandy Mamoli, Pieter van der Meché, Johanna Rothman, James Shore, and Karen Stephenson.

The members of the Supporting Agile Adoption initiative of the Agile Alliance made a great contribution to our work as both creative thinkers and as a sounding board. Thank you: Eric Abelen, Ray Arrell, Bjarte Bogsnes, Jens Coldewey, Esther Derby, Almir Drugovic, Hendrik Esser, Israel Gat, Don Gray, Michael Hamman, Jorgen Hesselberg, Anders Ivarsson, Bill Joiner, Boris Kneisel, Diana Larsen, Pieter van der Meché, Claudia Melo, Heidi Musser, Jaana Nyfjord, Ken Power, Michael Sahota, George Schlitz, James Shore, Dave Snowden, Rhea Stadick, Kati Vilkki. In this respect we also want to thank the Agile Alliance for supporting this initiative.

Special thanks to Katja Gloggengießer for all the great illustrations! Kudos to our early readers Christine Maßloch and Ramona Braddock Buck for the feedback and to Mario Lucero for inspiring us by his artwork.

Next we want also to thank all the participants who guided us with their questions and discussions in the right direction. Kudos to the workshop participants at: Agile 2016 and the ones from Agile India 2017: Vipin Agarwal, Syed Shabid Ali, Ravi P Ayyar, R Muni Yugandar Babu, Chandrakanth Biradar, Lalatendu Das, Sharath Desai, Manish Dureja, Thiyagarajan G G, Srikanth Ganugapati, Hari Iyer, Prasad Kabbur, Tarek Kaddoumi, Vijaya Kalluri, Satish Khot, Hari Kiran, Suneetha Konda, Guruprasad Krishnan, Seema Kumar, Ganesh T M, Sandy Mamoli, Shweta Mohindru, Uma Naidu, Sita Pun CSM, Divya Rajanna, Suman Ramaswamy, Mr. Shrey Razdan, Vasudevan A S, Balaji Sathram, Prashanth Shidlaghatta, Sunit Sinha, Surender Subramanian, Uday Tiwari, Mihir Ranjan Tripathy, Rajiv Tuli, Jatinder Verma, Chandar VR.

And finally we acknowledge our partners Ramona Braddock Buck and Nicolai Josuttis for their patience and ongoing support.

Introduction

Companies in general have a need for speed, face frequent market changes, deal with individual (and not general) needs of the customers (which demands individualizing products), struggle finding and keeping talent (which is even harder with the Millennials, who haven't grown up in hierarchical structures), and find that the digital revolution means that there is hardly any place where software isn't the disrupting factor independent of the industry's original focus.

Many companies are successfully using using some form of a process known as Agile development for information technology (IT). Agile has dramatically boosted software project completion rates while also allowing product decisions to be more nimble and accurate. Given this success, there have been attempts to apply agile concepts to parts of organizations that have nothing to do with software development, but only with limited success. They end up awkwardly using agile tools designed for software production for totally different kinds of work, e.g. by the board of directors using a "daily standup" meeting for synchronization instead of a traditional status meeting.

If we can all learn to apply agile-like concepts to our whole organization, we'll achieve similar revolutionary benefits across the board rather than only in the engineering department. And, we mean all companies and organizations from a bank or manufacturer to charities supplying food to the homeless.

To extend agile-like concepts, it is important to have a holistic view of the company (or organization) not excluding any parts. The holistic view has to address two challenges: surviving (and driving) intense disruptions as a company and expanding agile methods to the whole company. As a recent survey by McKinsey discovered: "Transforming companies to achieve organizational agility is in its early days, but yielding positive returns." (see McKinsey survey) Their survey further found that "[...] companies have higher aspirations for agility. Three-quarters of respondents say organizational agility is a top or top-three priority on their units' agendas, and more transformations appear to be on the way."

Both of these facets, the current challenges for companies and the need for implementing Agile beyond IT, demand guidelines for implementing company-wide Agility.

After researching, we found lots of recent, independent developments that attempt to address these challenges.

> We want to report what we found, and we admit that we felt overwhelmed by what is out there. However, we don't want you to feel overwhelmed, too! So, we suggest that you read this book with the expectation that you'll see a number of probably unfamiliar terms. Celebrate the newness without the ambition of mastering it all! You will definitely benefit from this book without juggling the terminology in your head.

At first, combining Agile and Sociocracy seemed really powerful, but the combination leaves gaps, e.g., in administrative support functions and in the people side: no consideration of passion. Beyond Budgeting and Open Space seem to be designed for addressing these gaps. In addition to these broad streams of development, we also found great insights in such specific tools and methods as Design Thinking, Lean Startup, Human Systems Dynamics, and Cynefin.

However, we also discovered in talking with various experts that if we asked them how to solve companies' challenges (basically how to implement company-wide Agility), we got an answer from within that expert's framework. For example,

- A Beyond Budgeting expert might say, "Stop fixing the budget annually, because otherwise you won't have the flexibility to react to frequent market changes."
- An Open Space expert might say, "You need to make space for what you don't know and can't control, for totally new things to emerge. If people are invited to follow their passion, you will be able to implement company-wide Agility, otherwise people will just do what they are asked."
- A Sociocracy expert might say, "You first need to resolve the power structure, because as long as you have a hierarchy defined as top-down you will not become agile."
- An Agile expert might say, "You need to start inspecting and adapting by using regular retrospectives in order to react flexibly, otherwise you will neither be able to learn from the market nor from within your company."

All of these perspectives are true, but the perspective is always from within the discipline. If pressed, they might assert that with their framework they would meet the goals of the other streams. But even then, they would address it within their framework and lose the richness the other frameworks provide. What's needed is the wider perspective that comes from synthesizing these frameworks. We've named the wider perspective BOSSA nova because it synthesizes the four streams: B = Beyond Budgeting, OS = Open Space, S = Sociocracy, A = Agile. As a phrase, "BOSSA nova" has different meanings:

- Translated from Portuguese it means "new wave" or new trend. And we think the synthesis is in some way a new wave that companies need to ride to address today's challenges.
- It is an upbeat style of music, a fusion of samba and jazz. What we are proposing is also a fusion, a fusion of the different streams.

- It is an intricate dance. Dancing always means adapting both to the music and your dance partner(s) as well as initiating new steps and even new music yourself. Dancers both react to their environment and affect it as their enthusiasm inspires the musicians and may even draw the audience into the dance. Although one person can initiate a BOSSA nova implementation, it will quickly become a team adaptation activity. And adaptation means you can't follow a recipe. BOSSA nova is not prescriptive; it flows with the situation at hand.

This book provides brief summaries of each of the streams without going into detail. The bibliography and the appendix point to details available elsewhere. However, you can use the ideas in our book immediately even if you have had exposure to only one of the four streams of development and / or if you are simply open to experimentation.

We took an Adaptive Action approach (from Human Systems Dynamics, see Eoyang & Holladay) to writing the book which suggests asking the questions "What," "So What," and "Now What"?

- **What**: In Part I we look at the "What," observations about the actual challenges companies are facing. These challenges are the need (the why) for new solutions. The Agile solution, rising with and partly causing the digital revolution has been a great success. However, attempts to solve the company-wide challenges by extending Agile practices to other kinds of work are proving inadequate. We sift through other strategies to find ones that could best address these company-wide challenges. We select four streams: Open Space, Beyond Budgeting, Sociocracy, and Agile - the BOSSA nova. Finally, to provide a foundation for a composite solution, we interpret the values of the Agile Manifesto for a company-wide context (see AgileManifesto).

- **So What**: This second Adaptive Action question asks for insights from observations. In Part II we address "So What," with our insight that the different streams describe the same values. We combine them to gain a richer, more complete picture. We develop that picture by diving into each foundational company-wide value (self-organization, transparency, constant customer focus, and continuous learning) to see what each of the four streams has to say. We conclude Part II by suggesting a new kind of company organizational diagram and a new way of viewing cross-functional teams.
- **Now What**: Part III focuses on the third question is "Now What." We explore how to implement BOSSA nova in a company. For practicality, we organize the insights of Part II into strategy, structure, and process. Noting that Cynefin recommends dealing with complexity by probing it, we suggest various probes that can be tried right away (see Cynefin). Part III concludes by verifying that the probes really address the challenges mentioned in Part I and by suggesting how to keep developing BOSSA nova in a fluent way. Part IV, the concluding part, looks at the place of companies in society.

As we move from section to section in the book, our tone changes. The changing tone reflects a kind a journey of insight, and we invite you to join us on the journey. The basic purpose of this book is to help you be open to exploring new ideas. The journey begins here!

If you feel so moved, please write a review about the book somewhere, for example, Leanpub, Amazon, Twitter, or your other favorite social media. Thank you so much!

I Gathering the Band

"It is quite a paradox how "western" business leaders praise democracy as the obvious and undisputable model for how to organize a society effectively. When the same leaders turn to their own companies, then their beliefs and inspiration seem to come from a very different place, from the very opposite ideologies." – Bjarte Bogsnes, Implementing Beyond Budgeting

"We cannot solve our problems with the same thinking we used when we created them." –Albert Einstein

---

This Part explores the Adaptive Action "what" question (see Eoyang & Holladay). What challenges are companies dealing with? What is the box we want to think outside of? What are the different attempts at addressing these challenges?

With the digital revolution, one notable stream of development, Agile, is pushing to expand beyond its core field - software development. We take a look at how Agile is addressing the challenges. We note that the attempts to make the Agile approach address a broad range of challenges, although well-intentioned, aren't succeeding the way Agile succeeds in the software world.

We start searching. We list and examine many other tools and attempts. We sift through these different attempts, keep a few set aside others.

And finally we generalize the values of Agile to make them usable company-wide.

1. Today's Challenges

Companies must become more nimble and flexible because they face a fundamental and growing challenge of complex, rapidly changing marketplaces, including digital disruption.

In companies' information technology (IT) departments a very successful approach to solving this challenge is Agile, as initiated by the 2001 Agile Manifesto (see AgileManifesto). But, companies trying to use Agile company-wide, beyond IT, are having limited success.

Hence, this Chapter covers two topics: - Challenges faced by companies in general. - Challenges faced by companies that are trying to extend information technology-based Agile approaches company-wide.

1.1 Challenges For Companies

Companies live in a VUCA world. VUCA meaning - volatile, uncertain, complex, and ambiguous. This VUCA is created, for example, by the war of talent, the changing demands of the Millennials and following generations, digitalization, the need for high speed to market, globalization, surviving and / or thriving on disruptions - just to name a few. This VUCA induces these companies to try to act in a more agile way - lowercase "a" meaning being flexible, fast, and adaptive - and wonder if they can use Agile - as defined by the Agile Manifesto or specific Agile methods like Scrum.

Complexity means that although we tend to create stories about cause and effect after something has happened, if a situation is complex, we can't really know what causes which effect. There is a lack of predictability; reality is hazy and full of possibilities to mis-read situations. And, although not every uncertain or ambiguous situation is automatically complex, every complex situation is at the same time both uncertain and ambiguous. In the past, companies created long-term plans and monitored if they were on track by using milestones.

A long-term plan today is outdated almost the day the plan is final-ized (or even before finished) because the market, the competitors and other influencing factors are changing so quickly. Planning assumptions seldom predict jumps in technology such as competitor breakthroughs, economic changes such as the unexpected recent Great Recession, and societal values. Thus, companies can not predict and plan anymore - at least not for the long-term, which is the reason why companies need a more agile way of planning.

Moreover, product solutions are far more complex than they have been before. Many companies see the need to partner with other companies, with their customers, or other communities as no one can solve these complex problems alone any more.

Several factors contribute to the challenge of VUCA, which we will examine in more depth below.

The solution is not necessarily obvious. For example, there is a current movement toward "no managers / no hierarchies", citing spiral dynamics theory of so called teal organizations (see e.g. Laloux). However, there is mounting evidence that although flat (large) organizations can increase creativity, they engender conflict, make difficult decisions more difficult, and drive away employees (see Guldner). So, the path to resolution of structure is not straight-forward. It must be more subtle and nuanced and consider several factors including size and people.

Size

Large groups of people generally seem to have a harder time being agile than small groups. Can an elephant be agile? Large corporations - often are forced to buy smaller companies that innovate faster than they can, but this strategy may still not solve the problem.

Lean Startup suggests that each company -small or large- should act like a start-up company to address the need for speed. Some large corporations (that are obviously not start-ups) address this advice by providing space within their corporations for start-up companies that they don't actually own. They may establish internal think-tanks (comparable to a start-up within the company). Or, they may buy start-ups and bring them in without changing their organizational "DNA." (In the past the parent company would typically try to change the culture of the purchased company.) While these strategies might make parts of the corporate elephant more agile, they don't address the whole. Hence, the challenge remains.

People

With the change of generations there are new challenges companies need to address. On the one hand it is harder to find skilled people who can deal with the problems the digital revolution is asking for, which means companies have to look for talent everywhere in the world and can not search for skilled people only locally.

And on the other hand, starting with the Millennials, following generations have grown up in "networks" and not in hierarchies. Whereas the generations before grew up in communities like the Boy Scouts or church groups, younger members of the workforce grew up in more ad hoc and less structured organizations, where an equal voice and following one's own passion is more important. Due to the wide usage of social media, it is more and more common to network and to speak up openly. People -not Millennials only-bring this behavior as well to work, which is not the typical behavior in traditional corporations. This network also results in different expectations regarding work places. Companies have to adjust to these new expectations - inviting people to follow their passion, providing equal access to necessary information, respecting everyone's voice, and not implementing hierarchies with autocratic power over one another. If companies are not preparing themselves for these challenges, they will struggle not only with recruiting skilled people, but also with keeping them.

Company culture also strongly affects innovation and supports or hinders change. As Anthropologist Karen Stephenson points out: "All cultures (including organizations and communities) are networks of trust; hierarchy is merely the scaffolding on which it hangs. Trusted networks are the greatest resistors to change. However, activating those trust networks is what catalyzes that very same resistance into sustainable change."

In general, typical human resource departments have elaborate systems of classifying work, creating job descriptions, and recruiting people to fill those jobs. A job description is a list of roles and responsibilities. Should companies first define jobs and then look for people? Or, should they look for people and then see what they can do? The latter question would perhaps lead to more innovation. Innovation seems to come from being a person with a meaningful, informed, passionate, equivalent voice and great social skills (see Duhigg) and not from someone fitted into a role like a clam in a shell.

Digital Revolution

As entrepreneur, investor, and software engineer Marc Andreessen mentioned in his often cited Wall Street essay: "Software is eating the world." (see Andreessen).

- In other words, there are fewer and fewer areas not infused with software. A simple example: many of the (traditional) car manufacturers nowadays do not regard themselves as car manufacturers but rather as software companies because the differentiator between one car and another is in the software. The same is true for banks and insurance companies. The consequence is that more and more companies need to internalize this different understanding of what is their core product.
- Artificial intelligence machines have now conquered realms once thought beyond machine intelligence such as the game of Go and poker. Automated drivers may soon steer our cars. Moreover, automating most parts of companies results in different consequences:
  - The required skills for the work force changes, the people need to be able to handle and program the automated processes.
  - It does seem likely that machines will soon take over many human jobs and that the only work left for human workers will involve innovation.
- Companies can no longer control how they are perceived from the outside. Social media in all its variants has the power to create a reputation for a company that is difficult to change. This enforced transparency requires a different relation with employees, customers and potential markets.

Collision of Values

A classic purpose of a firm is to maximize the shareholder value. The ultimate measure of a top executive is the current stock price. Executives are tied to that measurement. Underlying this measurement is the idea that the ultimate control of a company comes from ownership rather than emergent dialog involving investors, customers and other stakeholders. In this traditional view, a company must be owned by someone rather than owning itself. For a company to thrive it needs to be able to adjust quickly to market demands and serve even individual customer needs. Yet, focusing on maximizing the shareholder value is often in conflict with focusing on these customer needs as Steven Denning pointed out at the Agile conference 2016 (see Industry Analyst Panel):

> "And if you are working on the team level it's hard to comprehend the idea that the purpose of a firm is to maximize shareholder value as reflected in the current stock price and that executive bonus is tied to that. What that drives is a drive to extract value for shareholders, which is the direct opposite to agile which is to create value for customers. And so when you have an organization at the top which is striving to extract value and teams at the bottom pushing in the opposite direction you have a continuous and deep and horrible friction. This idea that the purpose of a corporation is to maximize shareholder value and current stock price is actually quite a recent idea and it only got under way in the mid 1980's and even Jack Welch has called it the dumbest idea even when he was a practitioner of it." – Steve Denning

Steve's quote describes a collision of values and structures. The challenge is to turn the "continuous and deep and horrible friction" into a win-win synthesis. A CEO might say in public that "our goal is to serve the customers." But the reality is that the Board is really focused on short term value for the shareholders. Thus, the friction remains hidden, which means it is harder to address. Sir Adrian Cadbury, citing Jack Welch former CEO of General Electric, recently commented on that friction (see Cadbury):

> "[...] 'your main constituencies are your employees, your customers and your products.' Maximising share-holder value has myriad detractors, who point out that

it is predicated on two false premises – that directors have a legal duty to maximise shareholder value, and that "the company" and "the shareholders" are one and the same thing. There is no shortage of potential alternatives, yet there remain stalwart apologists too – particularly in the financial and accounting world."

This collision of values may be the biggest factor inhibiting companies' ability to cope with our rapidly changing world. In Chapter 2 we explore existing strategies for resolving this conflict.

Summary of Challenges for Companies

The VUCA world creates many challenges for companies. These challenges ask the company to become more agile - in the sense of being more flexible and adaptive. Hence, almost naturally companies are looking for an Agile approach (as defined by the Agile Manifesto) to increase this flexibility and adaptability. As we'll see in the second part of the Chapter, Agile is one step, but it bogs down when applied company-wide.

1.2 Challenges With Expanding Agile

The Agile "movement" started with the desire to develop software more effectively. A milestone was the Agile Manifesto, published in 2001 (for details look at AgileManifesto). With the success of Agile methods for software and with software being almost everywhere - Agile is now being applied outside the field of software development. This application outside its birthplace has several consequences and raises many questions.

Difficulties with Agile at Scale

- Agile started off with single teams. Now also large development efforts want to benefit from the Agile approach, which means that Agile needs to be scaled up. So even inside the software or rather information technology (IT) field, big software projects and even whole programs are also using Agile. Different frameworks (such as SAFe, LeSS, Disciplined Agile Framework, Nexus - also referred to as Scaled Professional Scrum, Enterprise Scrum) have been developed that help scaling Agile this way. Most of these frameworks are highly complex and prescriptive ways of operating, meaning that they don't represent fundamental principles (see Jacobsen et.al.). They use the knowledge, e.g. from Scrum and Kanban, mix it together and apply it at a grand scale from development team to the program level. Also scaling approaches that are not built up as a framework but scale-up the Agile principles do not address how agility can be applied company-wide (see Eckstein and ScaledPrinciples). They focus on scaling one team to several teams but don't say how these teams are embedded in the overall company in an agile way. Finally, the prescriptive nature and the focus on the internal organization are contrary to the very spirit of agile, which is emergent and focused externally on delivering value to the customer (see Denning.) Yet, it is important to be aware that the foundation of Agile - the Agile Manifesto - doesn't limit the approach to only one team anyway.

- And now that Agile is applied outside software and IT answers are needed to what does it mean to be agile e.g. in Human Resources (HR), in marketing, in sales, in legal and how should those different departments be connected? Or should companies rather dissolve these departments?
- Scaling Agile to projects and programs has a profound effect on management leadership. Are the fundamental legal concepts such as exclusive control of corporations by shareholders still appropriate? From a broader perspective, the exclusive control of corporations by shareholders seems to create challenges for all companies not just those using Agile. We look deeper at this concern in Chapter 2.

- There is no single form of agility that applies to all teams, and none of these forms or variations address the following challenges regarding what company-wide Agility means for:
    - Organizational structure: Should there be a hierarchy using agile, a matrix, a network, or something else?
    - How budgeting, legal governance, or reward systems should work in an agile way?
    - Constantly focusing on the customer: This may be a particularly hard question if the shareholders are expecting quick return on investment.
    - Concept: There is no generally accepted definition of agile in a company-wide context. Does it mean transparency? Doing retrospectives (a meeting at the end of a period of work to capture lessons learned) and learning from them? Certain ways of acting such as self-organizing or eliminating managers? Using Kanban/Scrum? If there is no self-organization, is there agile?

Attempts at Company-wide Agility

All these questions need answers. There are various attempts to answer some of the questions:

- For example, there are a few companies experimenting with doing Human Resources and marketing in an agile way as well as applying business agility[1] cross-departmentally (see also AgileHRManifesto and AgileMarketingManifesto).
- There are companies whose management teams use Sprint backlogs for organizing and Daily Scrums for synchronizing their work. Even at the board level, sometimes Daily Scrums or retrospectives for capturing learnings are used.
- For interconnecting different teams there is the old approach of Scrum of Scrums, a meeting where representatives of

---

[1]https://businessagility.institute/

different teams synchronize on mutually important matters. The meeting shows the value of interconnections between teams even across projects, programs, or departments (if implemented broadly).

- A different approach for interconnecting teams (mostly within one project or program) are cross-team retrospectives. Thus, similar to the Scrum of Scrums, one or two people from different teams meet to reflect on the outcomes and their collaboration and to decide on necessary adjustments. (see Eckstein, Larman & Vodde)

- And then there is the other approach for doing cross-team work, which relies on self-organization. So, there is no particular answer but rather the confidence in the following principle from the Agile Manifesto: "Build projects around motivated individuals. Give them the environment and support they need, and trust them to get the job done." For example, one of the frameworks called LeSS (short for Large Scale Scrum), relies on this principle for creating the overall architecture with e.g. ten teams. Thus, LeSS trusts that the teams will find a way to agree on an architecture, for example, by electing representatives of each team, who will then decide on an architecture in a meeting. (Larman & Vodde)

- Moreover, there are all the before mentioned different frameworks for scaling Agile beyond a single team (see SAFe, LeSS, Disciplined Agile Framework, or Nexus).

Yet, there is no holistic perspective on company-wide Agility that addresses what agile means for the company's structure, strategy or overall processes. And neither are there any explanations as to what core agile values like self-organization, transparency, constant customer focus, continuous learning, or even feedback mean for a company so that it can be agile.

Summary of Challenges with Expanding Agile

Currently there are many fragmented approaches to the challenge of applying the Agile Manifesto company-wide. The attempts to expand agile company-wide have encountered conflicts around values and structure, the traditional stockholder value focus versus an egalitarian and customer focus. Also, the lack of a comprehensive theory of governance makes it difficult to develop new methods in a coherent way.

1.3 Summary of the Overall Challenge

While companies are recognizing that they exist in a volatile, uncertain, complex, and ambiguous (VUCA) world, there are no overarching concepts in terms of strategy, structure, and process to guide them in coping. There is a negative impact on people. For example, Millennials are frustrated because they expect to be involved in decisions and able to follow their passion, use what they know, and do what they see as important. People feel restricted by job descriptions which ignore their full potential.

Corporations today serve primarily to maximize shareholder profit, but this value framework is colliding with their ability to cope with rapid changes in technology and information overload.

Unclarity about how to expand the Agile Manifesto to company-wide agility has led to many fragmented and unsatisfying attempts.

So, whether we look at the challenges with generalizing agile company-wide, or look at the challenge of companies becoming more agile, we arrive at the similar problem statements:

1. Existing concepts cannot be directly applied to company strategy, structure, or process in the VUCA world.
2. Companies make decisions from the top down, but often people at lower levels who are closer to the realities of the

product or market have valuable insights that are currently ignored.

3. There is a collision of values underlying shareholder interest in short term profits and a focus on the needs of customers.
4. For a company to be agile, all departments must be agile; however, existing agile systems struggle when applied to non-engineering departments.

Solving these problems is what this book is all about.

2. Tuning the Instruments

In Chapter 1 we looked at what are the problems that companies and Agile practitioners face.

We are aware of historical developments such as "socio-technical research" as well as much more recent developments, and we sorted through them to select the most helpful. There is so much going on that we are sure that we missed some exciting developments because as we wrote the book we kept running across new activities.

After selecting four of the most promising developments we look at the principles and values of each. We pay particular attention to the Agile Manifesto and interpret the values so that they are easier to apply company-wide.

2.1 Developments We Considered

There are lots of developments related to the problems summarized in Chapter 1. In researching this book we looked closely at a number of recent developments:

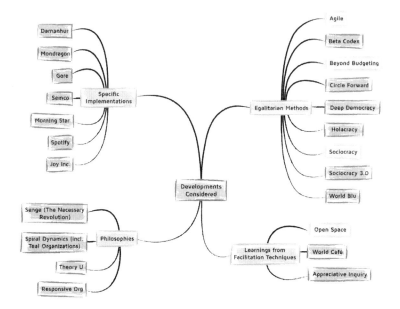

Development Streams Considered

2.2 Tools For Analysis

There are many diagnostic tools available for analyzing organizations. We kept several in the back of our minds such as the Viable Systems Model and Agile Fluency™ Model (see Beer and Agile Fluency.)

 A reminder of our earlier note: we are mentioning these technical methods so that you are aware that they exist and can investigate further if you want. They are only eddies in the main stream of this book.

We mostly relied on tools that focus on dealing with complex change such as Cynefin and Human Systems Dynamics.

- Cynefin - is a knowledge management model for describing problems, situations, and systems (see Cynefin and Snowden). The model defines a typology for different contexts that help to find a matching explanation and / or solution for the situation at hand. The originator, David Snowden of IBM developed this framework for explaining the evolutionary nature of complex systems - including their inherent uncertainty. Cynefin is based on research into complex adaptive systems, cognitive science, anthropology, narrative patterns, and evolutionary psychology. A great value of Cynefin is that if you deal with a complex situation, it explains why you can't follow recipes or do detailed analyses to understand the situation, rather you need to experiment (probe). Cynefin will become an important tool in Part III.
- Human Systems Dynamics (HSD) - is a collection of models, methods and tools for complex adaptive systems. It is grounded in inquiry and takes uncertainty and unpredictability into account by integrating complexity theory. For example, for staying in inquiry, one of the HSD models - Adaptive Action - inquires (see Eoyang & Holladay): *What* (for understanding the situation at hand), then *So What* (for generating insights), and finally *Now What* (for deciding what to do and evaluating the outcomes of the experiment). After the result of the *Now What* has been implemented (and outcomes experienced), it is time to initiate the next round by asking *What* again. In terms of understanding human systems, which are a complex, HSD inquires:
    - What defines the *Container*, which is what brings a specific group of people together?
    - What are the *Differences* - within a *Container* or between another one?
    - What are the *Exchanges* within a *Container* or with another one?

This heuristic is fractal, which means it repeats itself on different levels of abstraction.

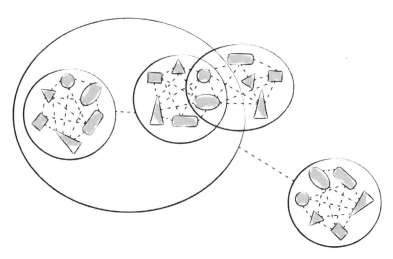

Human Systems Dynamics: Containers, Differences & Exchanges

To review each of the streams of development in the list, we examined how each stream of development will succeed in addressing the challenges outlined in Chapter 1 and its practicality without being too restrictive (meaning keeping it simple and pragmatic). All developments address some part of an out-of-the-box solution, some more so than others. We gave particular weight to solutions that can incorporate the various insights of these solutions in practical ways.

2.3 Considered But Didn't Use

We looked at lots of developments and decided not to go into company-specific ones like *Gore, Spotify, or Morning Star.* You might want to use them as recipes, but beware because they are context specific. We also decided against philosophies like *Senge, (Organizational Learning), Theory U,* and *Responsive Org* which present wonderful ideas, but don't really provide concrete advice (see Senge et.al, Scharmer, and Responsive). We started to classify Semco in this category but were intrigued to find that Semco has launched the Semco Style Institute. According to our review, the Institute offers variations of Open Space and Beyond Budgeting. Semco is just one of the examples of many developments that are bubbling up; it's hard to keep up!

Insights from Anders Ivarsson, Spotify

Spotify has become well known for our way of working and especially our way of structuring our product development teams - commonly referred to as the "Spotify Model". Although it was never meant to be a model or something others would try to copy or emulate, it has almost taken on a life on its own and there are now hundreds of companies claiming to run the "Spotify Model" or at least copying big parts of it.

When we wrote the original paper on Scaling Agile at Spotify and in later publications (eg videos on our engineering culture) we covered many topics - technical, process, culture, values, etc. Yet the one thing that people seem to remember and certainly the one they most often copy is the team structure - squads, tribes, chapters and guilds.

There are many strengths in this separation between delivery (squads, tribes) and mastery (chapters, guilds) - and we hear from many companies where only introducing this change has been valuable to them. But many companies are also struggling with these changes or aren't seeing big benefits from doing it.

I think it's interesting to understand why this happens - why a simple change in team structure can have a big impact on some companies, while others struggle to even get there, let alone get any benefits from it.

What I see at Spotify is that many aspects of our product and workplace are well aligned and reinforce each other.

- We have a high-trust, safe-to-fail culture that easily allows team autonomy.

- We have a product that is possible to slice into separate parts - allowing product teams to work on different priorities and in different cadences.
- We have a technical platform of micro-services and fairly modularized code - allowing teams to work on, build, ship, maintain and operate their part of the experience without requiring too much synchronization with other teams.
- We've kept evolving and experimenting with the best way of making company-wide priorities - aiming to find a good balance between working together on shared goals and getting bottom-up innovation and speed.
- Even our physical workspace has reflected our focus on teamwork and co-location.

The point here is that the team structure itself is not a silver bullet (duh - never is), but rather the team structure works well for us because it is well-aligned with our culture, our technical architecture and platform, our product, and even our workspace.

When you only take a part of this and apply to another context - you might see much more friction. If your organization is dealing with one big and convoluted codebase for the whole product - it'll be hard to give teams full autonomy. If you are working on more products than you have teams, giving each team a clear mission will be harder. If you operate in a heavily regulated sector with strict demands on accountability and decision tracking it might be hard to achieve a safe-to-fail culture and full team autonomy. If you only work on one technology stack (e.g., only web development) it might not make sense to split out different chapters and guilds.

We sometimes see this effect within Spotify as well - at least in the small. I was coaching a team working on a new area, and the team grew quickly to the point where we needed to split into several teams. After some discussions we found a vertical split of the team into three teams that each owned a slice of the experience. From a mission perspective the new teams were reasonably autonomous - they could make product and user experience (UX) decisions without always involving each other and could work on separate priorities. However, the backend system hadn't been built with a team split in mind and wasn't modularized enough, which led to three teams working on the same system - often running into each other, and requiring a lot of coordination between the engineers working on the same code. After a refactoring effort that split the system into smaller services that could be worked on independently and owned by one of the new teams, they were able to move much faster and actually get the benefit of their new missions and team autonomy.

Just as Spotify has worked hard to make all aspects of product development align well and work together - I see Jutta and John in this book exploring methods and processes that will work very well across the whole company. By combining these methods that cover different ways of running a company in a modern and more agile way, they are finding that together they can be more than the individual methods on their own - specifically because they are aligned and work well together, rather than causing friction and working against each other.

We looked long and hard at *Spiral Dynamics* (orange, green, teal organizations, etc.) popularized by Fredric Laloux's book *Reinventing Organizations*. In the end we decided not to explore it in depth because is is more of a set of explanatory categorizations than pragmatic work-a-day tools.

We looked for original, root methods where there is literature by many people. Thus, we picked Sociocracy over *Circle Forward, Holacracy, and Sociocracy 3.0* (see Circle Forward, Robertson and Sociocracy3.0). We also chose Beyond Budgeting rather than *Beta Codex* for the very same reasons (see Beta Codex).

We reviewed the history of approaches to management beginning with Mary Parker Follett in the 1920s and the Hawthorne experiments in the 1930s (Follett and Emery & Trist) that overthrew Taylors' mechanistic views of management and started a long train of development that involves understanding the role of people and technology in management. Sometimes referred to as socio-technical systems, these methods tend to be long-term oriented. They have a holistic organizational view and consider both the technical and the humane/social perspective. One of the key insights was that semi-autonomous and self-determined groups that work in a self-organized way together on a larger task are more successful than separating the larger task at first and assigning the tiny bits to individuals. We did not focus on socio-technical methods per se because we felt that this line of organizational development research, although still promoted by some under the term "socio-technical," has largely been subsumed in the other, more recent practices we mention.

We also favored developments that have been applied in general ways. For example, we are aware that some companies are trying to use Open Space company-wide because of its similarity to how Open Source communities (e.g. GitHub or Linux) are organized. This approach is also referred to as "Inner Source." We are not aware that anyone is trying to use *World Cafe* or *Appreciative Inquiry* as a method for organizing their company, and so did not include them (see Brown and Cooperrider).

Similarly, we looked at facilitation processes. *Deep Democracy* is a name coined in South Africa (see Deep Democracy) during the transition from apartheid to democracy. As later developed by psychologist Arnold Mindell, it focuses on our voices, states of awareness, and frameworks of reality to create a dialog in which every voice matters. Its primary use seems to be helping groups resolve entrenched conflicts. Other methods of this conflict resolution genre include Restorative Circles, Nonviolent Communication, and mediation (see Restorative Circles and Rosenberg). While we certainly think there is much value in these collective thinking methods, they do not go beyond facilitation to offer advice on how to structure power or conduct day-to-day business. We are unaware that anyone is attempting to run a company based on these methods.

We also studied *World Blu* (see World Blu). Traci Fenton has done wonderful empirical work documenting effective participative management practices, and companies that qualify for World Blu certification seem to do well on the bottom line. Readers may well want to study it further on their own. However, we decided not to explore it in depth because it doesn't articulate specific recommendations for combining complex systems and complicated systems, and it doesn't provide a theory of power, e.g., it doesn't appear to recommend legal structures that would underpin World Blu principles. As such, it doesn't seem to have anything to add to the problems articulated in Chapter 1.

Finally, another development worth mentioning is co-ops. *Mondragon*, initiated in the Basque region of Spain, has had notable success in reducing income inequality by articulating a cooperative approach to organization. It has successfully exported its methods to various parts of the world. Again, we note that readers may want to familiarize themselves with Mondragon's offerings, particularly training for co-op managers available online through Mondragon University. We did not choose to include Mondragon in the developments that will receive close attention because the co-op model limits the possibilities of venture capital participation in companies, thus avoiding rather than solving the conflict of values challenge noted in Chapter 1.

2.4 Converging Streams

After we completed our research, we decided to use Agile as a base for solving its own challenges because it has had spectacular industry acceptance over more than a decade. Also, the values defined by the Agile Manifesto seem to address the current challenges of companies that we explained in Chapter 1.

However, it was also clear that the values of the Manifesto need to be translated to address these company-wide challenges. To define the translated values, we decided to incorporate three other streams of development for improving organizational design including:

- Beyond Budgeting
- Open Space
- Sociocracy

We also used other development streams to define the translated values in limited ways such as Lean Startup and Design Thinking.

We do not claim to be in-depth experts in all the developments listed in the beginning of this Chapter. However, in preparing this book we did do a broad search on what's out there to be sure that our choices for a solution make sense. We concluded that a confluence of Agile, Sociocracy, Beyond Budgeting, and Open Space holds the most promise to be an integrative and pragmatic solution. These four streams offer the necessary comprehensive strategy needed to create a "general theory" of agile for company-wide operations (and even eventually for society).

These four streams all offer valuable approaches to the challenges discussed in Chapter 1. They have similar values and principles. Yet, they also complement each other by supporting company-wide Agility from different perspectives.

Now we will overview these four streams of development and provide more detail in subsequent Chapters. Please bear with us while we lead you through a bit of thick forest. ;-)

Beyond Budgeting

Beyond Budgeting was not so much created as discovered by a world-wide network of Chief Financial Officers (CFOs) who collaborated and extracted the values and principles that support the Beyond Budgeting concepts. They observed what makes companies successful from a financial and human resources (HR) perspective. The earliest implementation of Beyond Budgeting was at the Swedish Handelsbanken in the late 1970s, about the same time that Sociocracy was developing. A network arose from that early work called Beyond Budgeting Institute (see BBRT). There have been a number of books written about Beyond Budgeting (see particularly Hope and Bogsnes).

The term Beyond Budgeting does not refer to budgeting only. Budgeting is a common tool used by traditional command and control management. "Beyond" means beyond that traditional management model. The main difference is the values of empowerment and adaptation over command and control. The transition from command and control to empowerment and adaption is supported by principles for leadership style. The main focus is to understand the difference between fixed and relative targets. This focus is not prescriptive and, like Sociocracy and Agile, tries to leave open many possibilities to apply principles, in this case the empowerment and adaptation principles.

For example, in command and control management, fixed targets refer to projects with limited budgets and also to the fixed targets that manage the performance of the employees. In both cases the fixed target is not meaningful because if we have a fixed budget and we find the market has changed and we need more money to be successful, we can't because the fixed budget is all that we have. And, if the market needs less money, we typically spend the allocated amount out of fear that we won't get the needed budget for our next project.

For example, in terms of targets for employees, consider salespeople with a fixed target of 100 units of a product. If the person sells 80 and the competitor has sold 120, the sales person probably hasn't done well. However, if sales are 80 and the competitor sells 50, the sales person probably did well. Or, if I see by November that I won't make my 100 units target, I will postpone sales until the next year to boost my sales for next year. And vice versa if I have made my 100 target, I will also postpone sales to help make my next year's target.

The CFOs who invented Beyond Budgeting discovered that fixed target setting whether for projects or individuals is bad for the company because it doesn't allow adaptation or focus on recently developing needs. All twelve Beyond Budgeting principles are derived from this observation and ensure that adaptation can happen (for a complete overview of the principles see Appendix). For example:

- Customers: "Connect everyone's work with customer needs." This is a clear request for establishing a customer focus throughout the whole company.
- Transparency: This principle asks us to "Make information open for self-regulation, innovation, learning, and control because only informed people can make adequate decisions." The heading of this principle calls already for transparency.
- Autonomy: This is similar to the agile belief that micro management will not lead to good results: "Trust people with freedom to act."
- Rhythm: It is a request to "organize management processes dynamically around business rhythms and events and not around the calendar year only." Learn from what's happening in and around the company and take that learning into account and make relevant adaptations.

Beyond Budgeting approaches company-wide agility more from the classical finance and HR departments and shows how these departments can inhibit or support agility through their policies. It addresses the traditional support functions of a company.

Insights from Bjarte Bogsnes, Statoil

Beyond Budgeting is a great and powerful management model with a somewhat misleading name. It is actually not so much about getting rid of the budget. This is just one of many consequences of radically changing traditional management, moving from command and control to empower and adapt. It is about taking reality seriously, both our business environments, and people in our organizations. It is also about creating coherence between what organizations preach and what they practice. It does not help to have Theory Y leadership visions when Theory X processes run the show (traditional budgets are a classic example), creating poisonous gaps between what is said and what is done. There are many great concepts out there addressing either leadership or management processes. Very few addresses both and the total picture like Beyond Budgeting does.

Many in the Agile community have understood that Beyond Budgeting is about enterprise agility. It can be an effective way of scaling agile, which is hard, often impossible, when relying on exactly the same frameworks and language that worked so well for radically transforming software development. Most executives and senior managers are not familiar with or do not understand Agile (and most do not play rugby), so don't be surprised if they think Scrum is some kind of skin disease! Beyond Budgeting offers something executives can relate to, even if they still might disagree.

Here lies also the reason why the adoption of Beyond Budgeting has been slower than Agile (or Lean, as another example). Beyond its broad approach of addressing both leadership and management processes, the model also goes straight to the throat of so many executive beliefs and privileges, in ways that Agile and Lean didn't for software development and manufacturing. The C-suite just observed faster projects and lower costs. Not threatening, and not scary, unlike how Beyond Budgeting has been viewed from day one.

My own Beyond Budgeting journey, as described in my book *Implementing Beyond Budgeting*, started more than twenty years ago. I was lucky enough to work for a CFO and CEO who were wise and brave people. When we proposed a new management model with significantly more autonomy (and no budgets), the response was curiosity and encouragement instead of fear and negativity. It was a big leap of faith for all of us. There was nothing called Beyond Budgeting back in 1995. The company (Borealis) and the model we implemented became one of the cases that a few years later inspired what became known as Beyond Budgeting. The biggest source of inspiration for this movement was of course Swedish Handelsbanken, a company we actually hadn't heard about in 1995. This was a time when "search" meant going to the library and calling people! Our first years were relatively "no budget oriented", but the leadership side became bigger for us along the way. When I switched from Finance to HR in 1998 it all fell in place for me.

My Beyond Budgeting journey continued when I in 2002 returned to Statoil, the Norwegian energy giant. Again, I was blessed with a wise and brave manager. It is no coincidence that Eldar Sætre today is Statoil's CEO.

The decision to jump was taken in 2005, and since then I have worked full time on implementation, and still do. People often ask how long it takes, and if we are "finished". No, we are not, and maybe we never will be. This is not a project. It is a journey, where we all get braver along the way. We are today having discussions that would have been very difficult to have back in 2005, some even impossible.

We have continuously deepened and broadened the Statoil model, which we call "Ambition to Action". This includes for instance close and coherent links to our HR processes, kicking out the calendar year where possible and where it makes sense, implementing dynamic (as opposed to rolling) forecasting, as well as integrating Risk Management. A fascinating discussion emerging right now is about targets. Can we simply do without most of them? Why do we need to set a target just because we measure? There are other and better ways of setting direction and evaluating performance!

So where is Beyond Budgeting today, almost twenty years after the movement started out? The short answer: in a very different and much better place. The interest is record high, in business, in academia and in the consulting business. More and more companies are implementing it. The Beyond Budgeting Institute now has partners in a number of countries, and the Beyond Budgeting community is bigger and stronger than ever.

As described in this great book, there are a number of other concepts and communities out there. We might come from different places and we might speak different languages, but we are all fighting the same enemy. The more we join forces, the stronger we will be. I don't care what we end up calling it. At some point, not too far away, we will all smile about the time when traditional management was mainstream, just like we today smile about the time before the internet. It is not that long ago!

Open Space

The official term is Open Space Technology; however, we'll use the popular term Open Space. It was discovered by Harrison Owen, who organized great conferences but observed that people enjoy the breaks the most (see Owen). During the breaks the participants have time to network, to talk about subjects that matter to them, for as long as they want, and with whom they want. From this insight Owen developed the following principles of Open Space (for a complete overview of the principles see Appendix):

- *Whoever comes is the right people*: In a break conversation nobody thinks of waiting for a specific person before starting to talk. The same is true for an Open Space session.
- *Wherever it is, is the right place*: Conversations in breaks can take place anywhere as can an Open Space session.
- *Whenever it starts is the right time*: There is no need to wait for a specific time, just like during breaks people talk to each other without controlling their watches if this is the right time to get started.
- *Whatever happens is the only thing that could have, be prepared to be surprised!*: As in a break people don't follow a specific process, they just go on with the flow.
- *When it's over, it's over (within this session)*: This is analogous to the first principle, meaning that whenever people feel they're done with a topic they switch to another one.

As Michael Herman, founder of OpenSpaceWorld.org[1], comments, "These aren't prescriptive, they are the results of thousands of little experiments. They are descriptions of how almost anything works... When it really works." (see Herman)

Based on these principles Open Space supports the following values:

- Self-organization is at the heart of Open Space. Anything can happen. Participants are invited to identify and address all the issues that they see as critical to whatever success or solution is needed. Companies like Valve use exactly this idea for defining and delivering products. Every employee can suggest a product (or service) idea and as long as other people join in (called open allocation), this idea will be followed-up. In other words, even delivering customer value is based on self-organization.

[1] http://openspaceworld.org/

- Passion and self-responsibility is expected of every participant in an Open Space. Going with one's own passion means that whenever a participant recognizes she isn't contributing or learning, the participant can go to another place to learn or contribute (this is called the law of mobility - originally named law of two feet).
- Empowerment is necessary to allow Open Space to happen because you will never know upfront what people will focus on or who will work on what or for how long. Especially leaders need to be aware that even they don't know everything and that they can rely on others in the organization for filling the gaps and gaining new insights. This way, the leaders can realize and acknowledge that everyone, including themselves, indeed care and want to change the situation for the better. To paraphrase Herman again, "There is only common sense: let the people who know the work best use what they know to maximize the satisfaction of everyone involved." Typically, trust then builds as everyone experiences the process.

The values support the principles as Michael Herman comments, "*Whoever comes is the right people* acknowledges that the only people really qualified or able to do great work on any issue are those who really care, and freely choose to be involved. *Whenever it starts is the right time* recognizes that spirit and creativity don't run on the clock, so while we're here, we'll all keep a vigilant watch for great ideas and new insights, which can happen at anytime. *Whatever happens is the only thing that could have* allows everyone to let go of the could haves, would haves and should haves, so that we can give our full attention to the reality of what is happening, is working, and is possible right now. And finally, *When it's over, it's over* acknowledges that you never know just how long it'll take to deal with a given issue, and reminds us that getting the work done is more important than sticking to an arbitrary schedule. Taken together, these principles say 'work hard, pay attention, but be prepared to be surprised!'" And not to forget, *Wherever it is, is the right place* ensures that any location can support the work of the group.

Open Space principles reflect the core of Open Source development, as for example in the development of the Linux system. For quite some time there were discussions about how the Open Source approach could be transferred from volunteer work to industry. And nowadays, there are a good experiences with structuring a company around these principles (see, e.g., GitHub, Valve, and Whitehurst on Open Organization).

Open Space supports Agile, Sociocracy, and Beyond Budget by giving simple, clear instructions for inviting self-organization emerge. It can be used, purely as a facilitation technique, in large gatherings, and its principles can also be applied with smaller groups in a variety of circumstances to help us get out of our familiar ways, even our familiar ruts. Open Space principles can act as a kind of catalyst, accelerating the pace of Agile, Sociocracy, and Beyond Budgeting methods.

Insights from Michael Herman, Michael Herman Associates

I learned about Agile software development in 2002, when Chet Hendrickson, Ann Anderson and the pioneers at Object Mentor asked me to facilitate an Open Space track for the Agile/XP Universe conference outside Chicago. As they explained Agile to me, I blurted out, "You're making software in Open Space!"

In both Agile and Open Space, we actively invite people to put all the most important issues and opportunities, features and tasks, and everything else on the wall. And then, iteratively, a few at a time, we do the work in self-organizing (more or less autonomous) groups. These approaches work in otherwise hierarchical organizations because they invite and support exchange: Managers trade control for active engagement, workers trade transparency (exposure) for autonomy.

In Open Space, it's possible to walk into concentric circles of sometimes hundreds of people with no pre-set agenda, because the Invitation puts a clear, purpose – an attractor, in complex adaptive systems terms – at the center of the work system. The invitation allows managers to step back from control, having given the work priority and direction. At the same time, it calls forth everyone else to learn and contribute as much as they can toward the larger, shared purpose.

Some years ago, the managers running a 900-person gasoline delivery logistics unit invited into Open Space more than one hundred of their colleagues, representing a wide variety of functions and levels, with this simple email message:

> *Your palms are sweating, everything looks more and more complex. You are being asked to do more with less and you cannot see the light at the end of the tunnel. You feel like the chaos is catching up with you... Does this sound familiar?*

> *A more adaptive focus, as opposed to today's purely operational approach, needs to emerge from within [the division] to enable a sustainable performance advantage so that we remain on the edge of chaos, this sweet spot for productive change, where order and disorder flow with discipline.*

> *Please join us in investigating together what this sweet spot would look and feel like at [place/hotel] on [two and a half days]...*

This language sprung from a book on "adaptive challenges." These were not just big, complex issues, they were questions that they'd never seen before, essential shifts that needed to be navigated for the first time. After a year of study and discussion, the managers had wrestled the unit's future into a list of 12 or 15 of these challenges. Now they were ready to invite the rest of the organization to try to solve them.

The night before the program started, we seriously debated whether or not the managers' list of adaptive challenges should be announced at the opening. I counseled against this, and finally they agreed. As soon as the agenda was created and the breakout sessions started, the managers all pulled their lists out of their back pockets to check the work of the group. Sure enough, to their great amazement and relief, ALL of their "adaptive challenges" were detailed there, in the dozens of issues posted on the wall.

The next day at our Morning News plenary check-in, a big upset bubbled out. There was a growing sense of doubt and frustration. One man put it something like this, "I think we are failing here. I've talked with other people and none of this stuff (on the wall) makes our palms sweat or keeps us up at night. I think we're not doing what we came here to do!" Many others agreed, but didn't know what to do.

After more than an hour of difficult conversation in the big circle, the group came to understand and start to believe that they were doing and addressing everything the managers had hoped and envisioned, exactly what the organization needed to move forward. What the managers saw as the biggest strategic challenges and threats, everyone else experienced as simply "the stuff we work to solve every day."

By the end of their meeting, all of the most important issues (for managers and everyone else, it turns out) were identified, discussed, documented and on the morning of day three were prioritized by the whole group, by voting. This self-organizing team of more than 100 people produced a prioritized "backlog" that everyone understood and was ready to go to work on, together.

Sociocracy

Sociocracy developed largely from the efforts by Gerard Endenburg to find an engineering approach to making companies more steerable (see Endenburg and Buck&Villines). He derived four cybernetic (cybernetics = science of steering and communication) principles (for a complete overview of the principles see Appendix):

- Circles,
- Double-linking,
- Consent decision-making,
- Electing people to roles and tasks by consent.

His intention was to describe a generic method based only on engineering principles and not encumbered by a value system or a particular philosophy. For example, a hammer is a generic tool - any person or organization can use it. However, Sociocracy does have a context. Gerard attended a Quaker school that reinforced the egalitarian values of his parents who founded Endenburg Electrical Engineering (Elecktrotechniek) Company as a living laboratory for trying out new management ideas. Sociocracy principles have the effect of empowering individuals in a company including all stakeholders: from shareholders, to the local community, to the physical environment. Everyone is empowered.

1. **Circles** exist because their participants have a common aim. An aim is a product or service that the customer understands and is attracted to. Thus, a circle will soon cease to exist if there is no customer focus because there is no longer a reason for the circle to exist. A circle refers to the team of people who are participating in the system that delivers value to the external (or internal) customer. Thus, a circle is a parliament of people who are working in the system that delivers value to the customer (products &/or services). They make policy

decisions that guide their own day-to-day operations. They meet in traditional operational meetings to coordinate those day-to-day operations.

Circles are treated as organisms. As such they must develop continuously, regardless of whether there is pressure or stress. Development means learning, teaching, and researching in interaction with the circle's aim. Each circle is responsible for planning its own development and the development of each of its members. By emphasizing individual and circle empowerment, a sociocratic circle helps its members learn how to learn from complexity (see Drago-Severson et.al).

2. **Double-linking** connects circles. "Sociocracy" means rule by the "socios" or "partners." "Democracy" in contrast is rule by the "demos," the general mass of people. Thus, Sociocracy is a subset of the concept of democracy - it is democracy that works in companies. Have you ever wondered why you can't vote for your supervisor in your company but you can vote for politicians such as the town mayor or legislator? If you can't vote for your leader, you are not in a democratic structure. Sociocracy's concept of double-linking solves this dilemma. Double-linking means that each circle elects a representative (someone not the boss) to sit in the next higher circle and participate fully in the policy decisions of that circle. Double-linking is a way to build feedback into an organizational structure. A critical point is that it is feedback that cannot be ignored because of the consent principle, discussed next. Double-linking goes all the way to the board of directors, meaning that an elected representative(s) from the staff/workers sits on the board with full power to participate in the board's decision-making.

3. **Consent decision-making:** In a circle meeting all partici-pants must have an equivalent voice so that accurate feed-back can emerge. Making a decision by people who are completely equivalent presents a challenge. There can't be a

single higher leader who resolves different viewpoints. We can't really expect agreement because we all have different perspectives, and what is agreeable to one person may not be "logical" to another. Sociocracy solves this conundrum through the concept of consent decision-making. A consent decision is not one that you unite with or agree with but one that you can accept (or tolerate). You consent if you have no reasoned and paramount objection to a policy proposal. All elements of any system must be able to "live with" (function in some way) in the system or the system will not work. For example, a car tire can withdraw its consent by going flat. Sociocratic consent decision making occurs only in circle meetings and follows recommended processes that have proven effective over time.

Note that while "consent" may sound "almost like consensus," it is actually quite different. For example, you can never reach a consensus decision with your car's tire. It is incapable of agreeing to anything. However, as an element in a system, it can withdraw its consent. For consensus, the typical question is if everyone is in favor of the decision, whereas for consent the question is if everyone "is able and willing to execute the decision" – this doesn't necessarily imply being in favor, yet accepting the decision (also referred to as having "no reasoned and paramount objection").

4. **Electing people to roles and tasks by consent** is a corollary of the consent principle. In the double-linking principle we mentioned that the elected representative participates fully in the process of electing the supervisor or manager of a circle. The recommended process asks for consent to a candidate whose name emerges in a self-organizing way from the circle. It does not rely on majority vote. Typically the selection process does not result in the familiar feelings of victory or loss but rather a perception of satisfaction that "we have together made our selection." The process is used to select

people for all major roles and responsibilities.

Sociocracy asks us to think in practical ways about such fundamental questions as "Do the company bylaws actually support complex, emergent thinking or are they an anachronism left over from the old ways of top down, command and control governance?" It makes us sensitive to out-of-balance power arrangements. Self-organization occurs only when everyone is empowered and attuned to customer needs. Because the procedures developed for implementing Sociocracy are effective across many kinds of cultures, people, and work, they bring a perspective that is generic.

Insights from Pieter van der Meché, The Sociocracy Group

Why should top management take an interest in Sociocracy? After 21 years of experience my short answer would be "Because it boosts the level cooperation amongst all stakeholders at all levels of an organization." Many organizations suffer from an 'us versus them' culture, from 'saying yes but not doing it' and from 'complaining without taking responsibility for the problem'. This dichotomy doesn't always show from the outside and especially not to top management because people do not feel safe enough to speak up. They fear running into a conflict with their leadership and the negative impact this might have on their careers. The downside of this conflict is that many good ideas, initiatives, insights and energy get lost. They do not even come to being.

As a top manager you want to know what really goes on in the hearts and minds of your company's stakeholders. And you want them to be able to attune their different perspectives into a coordinated effort to achieve the organization's goals. That is exactly what a sociocratic decision making structure helps them to do. Better than any other decision making structure.

I have trained many general circle meetings, the place where top management decides company wide policy together with the leadership and representatives of the next lower management level. I have seen often how the sociocratic approach helped turn very antagonistic initial positions, into shared decisions where all circle members felt truly committed.

I remember a large department of a college where they had to decide on promotions of staff. There was money for only five because of a budget cut, but team leaders had already promised up to 20 people a promotion. What to do? Who would get promoted and who not? After two rounds in which team leaders strongly defended their people's promotions and tried to shove the difficult decision into the hands of top management, someone started to think out loud how he would handle a salary cut at home. "I would try to save money to cut my expenses. I would not talk of buying a bigger house or more expensive holidays. Why would I act different in the office." That was the trigger for an idea to emerge: no promotions at all because of the budget cut and not wanting to favor some employees over the others. When this proposal was put to consent, a few team leaders objected. "I have a person in my department that is doing a fine job for years but never received the salary that goes with these tasks. I cannot come back to him and tell him he will not receive the promotion that would do justice to the level at which he is actually functioning for quite some time."

During the opinion forming round that followed many acknowledged that there were some cases of people that were badly underpaid. So, everyone consented to an addition to the original proposal: team leaders who thought they had such hot cases in their team could explain the circumstances to the circle. If the case for a promotion was clear to everyone, there would be a raise. If it was murky (for example, unanswered questions) there would be no raise. Three cases were put forward, one got consent. The group left the room united and feeling empowered to explain and execute the decision. So they did.

Interestingly the group did not get stuck, keep negotiating with management for more money, or set out to achieve the maximum number of promotions. Instead, they focused on the common goal: having a financially sustainable department. They reconsidered their own opinions and views on the basis of arguments and information shared in consecutive rounds where each had an opportunity to speak up. They developed a common understanding. But most important, the responsibility to decide on the solution was in the hands of each individual participant. It is this combination of being able to decide for yourself what you consider within your range of tolerance or not and the shared responsibility for solving the problem together which stimulates participants to listen carefully, reconsider their opinions, and focus on the common goal.

For the consent principle to be effective, 'social safety' is important. Participants must feel free to use their consent during the circle meeting to be able to correct decisions that are not acceptable to them. Even if these corrections raise lots of tension. All attempts to impose rules to limit the use of the consent principle during circle meetings undercuts its effectiveness. Examples of such limiting rules include, "You may only speak from your 'role'; or, "You are limited in the topics you're allowed to talk about - don't talk about strategy issues because that's the leader's domain." Such rules, when used as absolute criteria, become a source of manipulation with many negative impacts on the level of cooperation.

Agile

The Agile Manifesto comes with a set of values and principles guiding company teams to improve their ways of developing software (for a complete overview of the principles see Appendix). Now that we are focusing company-wide, beyond software team level to address the full spectrum of work, we need to translate the values of the Manifesto that they become applicable for the whole company.

The following interprets these values in a company-wide context (items in quotes are from the Manifesto):

1. "Individuals and interactions over processes and tools": In its original software context, this value means that an agile team has to find its own specific process (and improving it over time) thereby helping to create business value for the customer. Thus, processes and tools have to support people and their interactions and not the other way around. Companies not using agile tend to have standard processes and tools that prevail regardless of the team needs. However, for a company-wide context, we believe that this value must reflect the need for the whole company to operate as a complex, emergent system. A complex system can only be guided by people (sometimes referred to "alignment for autonomy"). Tools do not emerge by themselves. To operate as a complex system the company must foster **self-organization** throughout.

2. "Working software over comprehensive documentation": Obviously, this statement refers specifically to software. It means that the truth is in the actual running system and not in the documentation that describes what the system ought to do. Consequently, the running system makes the actual progress transparent and only with this knowledge can the team (and its stakeholders) make informed decisions. Participants in our workshop at the Agile India conference in 2017 suggested "visible delivery," which we initially liked a lot. But, upon reflection, every part of the company does not necessarily create a tangible deliverable. Further, the term "visible delivery" emphasizes the outcome not the whole process of producing a product or service. Hence, "working software" refers to "what is actually happening" regardless

of the kind of work being done and can include a feeling of exposure of personal vulnerability. Transparency means ability to access information and not necessarily "clarity." For example, knowing that things are chaotic means the situation is transparent but probably not very clear. **Transparency** must be in place company-wide - not just within a team using an agile approach.

3. "Customer collaboration over contract negotiation": Contracts are important but they don't ensure that we are creating the right product. A team building a product (or providing a service) must keep in constant touch with external (and internal) customers to find out what they really need. In a company-wide context, it means finding imaginative ways to keep in constant touch with customers to ensure that your product or services truly meet their needs. The process of hunting for customers, establishing relationships, and growing them doesn't just happen. The interests of both the customer and the company providing the service or product need to be aligned. If the interests are aligned, the company naturally will keep **constant customer focus**, which is key for the whole company. Everyone must develop a deep understanding of their customers regardless of their role in the company.

4. "Responding to change over following a plan": In its original software context, teams create a plan, but the plan is not as important as the planning. Getting feedback about customer needs, collaboration with colleagues, and reviewing technical results, etc., must be responded to. The response means learning from feedback and perhaps developing new methods, more effective behaviors, and adjustments in plans. It's about not knowing and not controlling what comes next, and making choices along the way. The learning can range from small improvements to transformative leaps to new systems. For a company to learn, every individual must contribute to enterprise growth, in the same way that a living

organism continually adjusts and develops. Therefore, **continuous learning** is fundamental for company-wide Agility.

Although there have been other translations of the Agile Manifesto for different reasons (see AgileHRManifesto, AgileMarketingManifesto, or ModernAgile), we believe that by translating the core values of the Agile Manifesto in this way, they can be applied to an entire enterprise. We are not saying we need a new Manifesto, we only want to make it more applicable to the whole company.

Feedback drives all four values - both the original Agile Manifesto values and the derived values for company-wide Agility. For example, "customer collaboration over contract negotiation" relies on getting and giving feedback to and from the customer as does constant customer focus. However, just saying "drink more feedback" is not enough, because it is too generic. To make it useful we need to differentiate and be more specific about the nature of the feedback. Self-organization, transparency, constant customer focus, and continuous learning can "thrive a company." They enable company-wide Agility.

These values are conditions enabling companies to survive and thrive disruption in the VUCA world that we can't deny or escape rather than formulas. Implementing these agile values company-wide is not straightforward, as we saw in Chapter 1 in the discussion of challenges with expanding agile. To make the values applicable we need the combined wisdom of other streams of development: Beyond Budgeting, Open Space, and Sociocracy.

Insights from Johanna Rothman, Rothman Consulting Group inc.

Agile is a Mindset, Values, and Principles

A mindset is the values, beliefs, and principles you hold that guide your actions in a situation.

An agile mindset means you value the collaboration and feedback in an agile team. You believe that small steps and frequent checking of progress will help. You believe that people collaborating together can deliver a terrific product. You use the agile and lean principles of collaboration, delivery, and transparency to guide your work.

Agile builds in adaptation to your projects and daily work. You can make this adaptation work if you adopt the growth mindset. When you work as a team, adopting the growth mindset, and the agile and lean principles, values, and beliefs, you often discover you can experiment and learn from your experiments.

The agile mindset is one that says, "What small experiment can I learn from and make progress based on the outcome?"

Consider this as a working definition to guide your selection of practices:

- You can deliver what you want (some form of value).
- You can deliver that value when you want.
- You can then change to the next most important chunk of valuable work.
- You learn from the previous work you did, both about the work and the process of doing the work.

That's not all agile is, but it might be a good working definition. If you work towards being able to deliver what and when you want, move to the next thing, and learn, you have the feedback cycles. (Please do review the agile principles behind the Manifesto.)

You might find these practices can increase your agile capabilities:

- Iterations, because they limit the work a team can commit to in a given time period.

- Kanban with work in progress limits, because they limit the work a team can do, and show the flow of work.
- Retrospectives because you learn from previous work.
- Standups if people work alone because they reinforce micro-commitments to finishing work.
- Pairing, swarming, or mobbing on work because they limit Work in Progress and help the team review work and learn together.
- Technical excellence practices from XP (extreme Programming), because they make changing the code and tests easier.

You don't need any of these to be agile. They help. You might find other practices to be more helpful in your context.

Remember, agile is a mindset of collaboration, transparency and delivery to guide your work. It's not about a specific framework or dogma. Agile approaches invite change inside the organization and outside, and they create a culture that helps people grow and succeed.

2.5 Summary

In this Chapter we evaluated different streams of development and examined which ones would best address the challenges of company-wide Agility posed in Chapter 1. We decided to focus on those streams that are simple, pragmatic, and not philosophical, company specific or derivative.

We chose the following core streams of development, listed here in the order of our mnemonic BOSSA nova:

- **B**eyond Budgeting because it addresses the necessary flexibility and adaptability of companies from a financial perspective,

- Open Space because it works with passion bounded by responsibility in a way that can multiply the effectiveness of the first three methods,

- Sociocracy because it puts feedback into the whole company structure and synthesizes the seemingly conflicting interests of shareholders and customers, and

- Agile because it has been so successful and accepted in the field of software development and beyond, especially important in the context of rapid digitalization of nearly all facets of business.

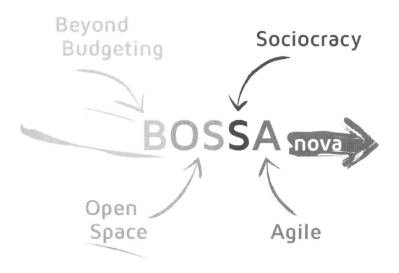

BOSSA nova Journey

We will later draw on the insights of other streams such as Lean Startup and Design Thinking because they offer innovative strategies for keeping super-creative people on track and focused on customer needs.

Each stream by itself contributes to greater flexibility and adaptiveness. In the rest of the book we will explore each of the four core streams individually in more detail and also how their confluence can support company-wide Agility.

The "nova" ("new" in Portuguese) refers not to any of the streams of development but to your journey! Implementing BOSSA nova means being on a journey without a final destination. In the beginning of Part III, we'll explore how you can start and stay on the journey.

II Improvising the Tune

"Which comes first, your people, your customers, or your shareholders? And I would say, it's not a conundrum. Your people come first, and if you treat them right, they'll treat the customers right, and the customers will come back, and that'll make the shareholders happy." – Jeremy Hope, Peter Bunce, and Franz RÖÖsli in the Leader's Dilemma.

In Chapter 2 we only looked at the value of each stream without worrying too much about how they are interrelated. In this Part we look at how they relate and support each other and fill in each other's gaps - the "So What" question.

Rather than developing a whole new framework (or coming up with yet another manifesto) and fitting all four streams into it, we decided it would be easier to start with one framework and add the other streams into it.

Because of the current importance of digital disruption (Andreessen: "software is eating the world"), we decided to start with the stream that has developed in the digital world, Agile and elaborate the values derived from the Manifesto for use in a company-wide context:

- Self-Organization
- Transparency
- Constant Customer focus
- Continuous Learning

Experience indicates that these values work in the real world. The values are a testimony to that experience and not a statement of a deeper belief system.

What we will do next is explore each of these values to see how each of the streams contributes to making it applicable company-wide. This approach means we are separating the perspectives knowing that we risk limiting the narrative. At the end of each value exploration, we provide an initial synthesis (or narrative) for the value. In Part III we take a holistic approach.

3. Self-organization

By "self-organization" we mean that a system (e.g. a team) does "it's own thing purposefully" without external control (see PrincipiaCybernetica). With people, self-organization seems to require that everybody is equivalent and has the opportunity to contribute something. Equivalence means everyone matters and they add their individuality to the collaboration. Even if the roles are very specific and very limited and people are very different, still the voice of everyone is required to achieve the common goal. Thus, although people are often very specialized in their roles they also play a big part in the whole and with their view. Everyone having a meaningful voice in the whole is a pre-condition for self-organization and emergent thinking to happen.

For example, in a scrum team, the whole team can negotiate the assignment in the planning meeting and can furthermore add their thoughts to a retrospective. In this way the team self-organizes and new ideas emerge. If only a few members were allowed to participate there would be bad estimates of what work could be done in the sprint and only limited insights about improvements to the process.

3.1 Challenges for Self-Organization

How can management tell everyone to self-organize? And what is the role of a manager in a self-organizing system? In a traditional organization the management is used to a command structure to tell the people what to do. That stops any self-organizing activity. The tasks given any group of people are usually so interlinked with other activities that they don't have enough autonomy to self-organize.

Or, if you are using a Tayloristic approach of cutting work into small pieces, the bits are too small to self-organize. If the capability, responsibility and task are separated (some to the manager some to the "managee"), self-organization cannot happen (see Emery & Trist).

Another challenge is that for a group to self-organize, every voice in the group needs to be heard. This is also true if self-organization is applied company-wide. However, conventional practices do not say how "hearing everyone voice" can be achieved.

3.2 Perspectives from the Different Streams

We now turn to the four different streams - Beyond Budgeting, Open Space, Sociocracy, and Agile for insights into how each of them approaches the concept of self-organization. Also, we add the view from Human Systems Design, one of the useful tools we cited in Chapter 2.

Beyond Budgeting

Beyond Budgeting emphasizes the importance of trust for autonomy in the principle 5: *Trust people with freedom to act; don't punish everyone if someone should abuse it.* This principle is based on the fact that conventional companies put a lot of rules and guidelines in place to control abuse and cheating. Consider, for example, common regulations for travel expenses like the kind of hotel or the travel class. These regulations often are written from a framework that assumes people will spend too much money unless they are controlled or bossed around. Instead of trusting a department or unit and dealing with the untrustworthy ones later, the culture mistrusts everyone. As Bjarte Bogsnes explains:

"As in so many leadership situations, there is a simple (but wrong) response and a more difficult (but right) one. Simple and wrong is about putting everybody in jail because someone did someone wrong. [...] The right, but also the more demanding response is to have that very firm talk with those involved, and let it have the necessary consequences. Trust is not about being soft." (Bogsnes, pos. 3131)

Setting up a trust culture leads also to fewer rules and regulations and therefore, to less micromanagement, hierarchical control, and bureaucracy, which is what the principles 2 and 4 are asking for.

- Principle 2: *Govern through shared values and sound judgement; not through detailed rules and regulations.* The shared values are the glue for a group of people to work self-responsibly together. Values guide more surely than any rules and regulations because they guide the whole person. Rules and regulations can only set a framework while values can guide from moment to moment.
- Principle 4: *Cultivate a strong sense of belonging and organise around accountable teams; avoid hierarchical control and bureaucracy.* Similar to Agile and Sociocracy, Beyond Budgeting defines a common goal - here being accountable for something - as a prerequisite for self-organization. Or in other words, if a group of people doesn't have a common goal they can't self-organize, because there isn't anything they can self-organize "around". And, encouraging a sense of belonging brings in the idea of both equality and inter-personal attunement that is the other prerequisite for self-organization.

Open Space

Open Space is based on self-organization completely. Open Space invites participants, to make the format fit the purpose. For example, there is a pre-defined time for a meeting to end, but it will be adjusted when it is clear how much time is actually needed: in other words, the work does not need to end just because the pre-defined ending time of the meeting has been reached. The underlying structure encourages anyone to suggest a topic and everyone to organize around the topics in ways and places most helpful for achieving the goals inherent in the topics. Individuals stay with the topic or chose to move to different topics, as moved by their interests and desires to contribute.

This format differs dramatically from traditional meeting culture, where:

- "qualified" people (often the boss) invite attendees,
- the "right" people are invited (often also defined by the boss), and
- the amount of time for the meeting is pre-defined (which typically means that the meeting endures exactly as long as pre-specified) even if it really could be much longer or shorter).

Therefore, Open Space relies on self-selecting teams to work to-gether (see Mamoli & Mole). This approach is the key differentiator from the other streams, in which the composition of the team, group, or circle has external influences. Once formed, the team then starts to self-organize. Whereas in Open Space people decide for themselves which team, group, or circle they want to join. Because individuals are the very best managers of their own experience, learning and contributing, Open Space gives people the right and the responsibility to make the right choices to self-organize around topics that need to be discussed or solved. Organizational Open

Space, in which companies organize themselves according to the Open Space principles, gives everyone the right and the responsibility to learn and contribute as much as they can, for the good of the whole organization or customers or some other collective and important purpose. And similar to the other streams - without a collective topic or rather common goal, no self-organization in Open Space will take place.

Sociocracy

Sociocracy draws on the insights of Nobel prize winner Ilya Prigogine to create a structure that supports self-organization. Prigogine saw that whether we're talking about gas molecules in a laser, grains of sand in the bottom of a creek, or a gathering of people, if you have elements of a system that are basically equivalent and introduce an outside force, the elements will self-organize. A laser requires an electrical jolt for the gas molecules to emit coherent light, the grains of sand require running water to self-organize into ripples, and a group of equivalent people need a common aim, the pressure of a customer's needs, to self-organize their work.

Equivalence means that though everyone is different, every voice must be heard. It is a critical requirement for human self-organization. Sociocracy uses the procedures of consent decision-making to create this necessary equivalence. A decision is made by consent when no one has a reasoned and paramount objection to the proposed decision. The processes for consent decision making do not ask everyone to begin by trusting each other but rather create a structure that builds trust over time.

Sociocracy adds one more concept: the idea of self-organizing at different levels of abstraction. Work naturally happens at different levels of abstraction. For example, in early spring a gardener might refer to a seed catalog to select the plants she will grow in her garden. She might make a sketch showing how she will lay out her garden plot. These activities are rather abstract. By late spring she will do the concrete work of tilling the soil, planting, and then weeding.

In a traditional organization the "abstraction workers" use a command structure to tell those doing the actual work what to do. That stops any self-organizing activity by the people doing the ("concrete") work because the required equivalence disappears and self-organizing can't happen. The figure below shows a typical traditional, top down governance structure.

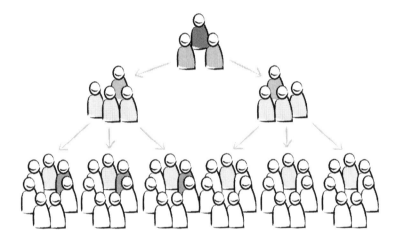

Top-down Governance Structure

Sociocracy uses a system of feedback from the "bottom" that can't be ignored to restore equivalence. Rather than a single command connection, abstract to concrete ("top to bottom"), there is a second power system that also creates a flow of power from concrete to abstract ("bottom to top"). This dual influence system is called double linking, meaning that at each level, in addition to the manager (who speaks from abstract to concrete), a person is elected to speak from the view of concrete to abstract. Each level is connected to the next level above and the next level below with two people, not one. Policy decisions at each level are made using consent by managers and the elected representatives for that level meeting as a policy circle. Adding the upward voices creates a circular hierarchy.

Circular Governance Structure

Agile

Agile links self-organization to *trust* in the individuals and their interactions. This linkage gives freedom for the teams to come up with a process that serves their needs and stops the company from dictating tools and processes that might not be the right fit for the actual purpose. The retrospective is the usual place where the adjustment of the process is happening. Moreover, leaders asked to trust the team members and to provide an environment so that they can create the customer value. (Comparc this as well to the 5th principle of the Agile Manifesto: Build projects around motivated individuals. Give them the environment and support they need, and trust them to get the job done.) Yet, all too often companies define rules and guidelines that slow teams down or rather hinder them in being successful.

As a prerequisite for self-organization, agile asks for teams to be cross-functional. A team can deliver a complete product only if all different perspectives on the product work together jointly. The delivery of a complete product (or complete functionality or user story) serves as a common goal for the team, which is another pre-requisite for self-organization. If instead, teams are set up according to functions, every team can only concentrate on its functional expertise, which leads typically to incompatible interfaces in the final product.

3.3 Additional Perspectives

Human Systems Dynamics (HSD) - is a collection of models, methods and tools for complex adaptive systems. It is grounded in inquiry and takes uncertainty and unpredictability into account by integrating complexity theory. HSD, defines three conditions for self-organization (see HSD and Eoyang):

- A **Container**, which is any human system that organizes around "something." The something can be a belonging, a delivery, a belief or anything the like as e.g. a nation, a service, or a religion.
- **Differences** that differentiate one container from another and creates tensions between parts within the same container. The tensions can be creative or destructive, i.e., conflictual tensions, depending on how they are regarded and handled.
- **Exchanges** that define the interactions between containers. This heuristic is fractal, which means it repeats itself on different levels of abstraction.

From this perspective self-organization can have many nuances. For example, if you have many like-minded people in a group (a container with a narrow focus) the self-organization may become easier. You may have observed this phenomenon in professional gatherings where everyone speaks the same jargon or in a family gathering where everyone shares a common history. However, if you have only like-minded people together (narrow container) the number of exchanges between groups will go up because every group will have a different output that needs to be reconciled with other groups. The differences between the groups will be sharper.

Thus, by varying containers, differences between containers, and nature of exchanges between containers, one can adapt the self-organizing phenomenon to the needs of the work to be done. The situation at hand decides what is more helpful in the moment.

Insights from Sandy Mamoli, nomad8

Snapper are a Transport Ticket Service provider from Wellington, New Zealand. While relatively small with just 60 employees they service clients all over the world.

Their journey started with Agile seven years ago, moved towards Holacracy and ended with a magic blend of Agile, Sociocracy, Holacracy and a dash of Open Space.

Agile

In 2010 I was part of introducing Agile to Snapper's IT department and parts of the business. The hopes for our agile adoption were to collaborate better across IT and to improve the speed and quality of project delivery.

Agile delivered to its promise: Snapper achieved better delivery and, most importantly, a culture of collaboration, respect and true passion for transport customers flourished. Over the last seven years they had achieved true agility where people live by the principles and are completely in control of how they work.

However, agile was restricted largely to IT and parts of the business. They still had a traditional structure with IT, finance, marketing and customer service teams. Collaboration between those teams was sometimes difficult and things could fall through the cracks.

Radical Organisational Re-design

In 2016 Snapper foresaw success and growth – and were well aware of the pitfalls involved in scaling up. So they wanted a foundation that would let them add people without adding pain.

That's when they read about Holacracy. They were drawn to its promise of better collaboration and thought it could supplement agile by providing a framework for the entire organisation. Radical transparency, decision making at the right level, and dynamic organisation all seemed right.

They were also attracted to the potential of baked-in continuous improvement. In Holacracy each team (circle) and role are responsible for their own development. As the CTO pointed out, if you have 50 people each making one small change a quarter, it adds up to 600 small improvements a year – and all through a cultural process driven by the people, rather than a top-down mandate.

Holacracy

I'd worked with Snapper in the past and they asked me back to help them introduce and embed Holacracy. We all went into it with an open mind.

We started with a strict implementation that followed the rules to the letter. We wanted to try everything as it was designed to be, and then make any changes from a position of knowledge and experience rather than because we found a practice too hard to implement.

We began to induct our circles: defining each circle's purpose, domains and accountabilities. So far, so good. I fully expected to be done in a month or so. How hard could it be?

Very hard, as it turned out. People found it confusing and didn't like the legal language and rigid rules that felt at odds with their organisational culture. And while most people understood why we were introducing Holacracy, they didn't have a clear picture of how things would work once it was in place.

Sociocracy

We saw potential in the ideas and goals behind Holacracy but it's easy to lose sight of the principles and become obsessed with the system itself when there are so many rules in the constitution. In agile terms it's like the difference between "being agile" and "doing agile".

When we face this problem in the agile world we resort to the agile manifesto and its associated principles for guidance. In the world of organisational redesign we discovered that the underlying principles of Holacracy were actually Sociocracy.

Focusing on the sociocratic principles allowed us to communicate the essence of the system and its desired behaviours to the rest of the organisation in a clear and concise manner.

It helped us improve our collaboration and making good decisions has become noticeably faster and easier. We think decision-making by consent rocks!

The system with its interlinked circles has provided visibility, which allowed us to see when something could be improved.

Open Space

With Sociocracy / Holacracy people realised that they had the power to improve the areas they worked in, and that once a problem had been identified it could be solved with input from many contributors. Those improvement projects were driven by people who chose to work on them, a type of self-selection into working groups. It formed our springboard into Open Space Technology.

Open Space's self-selecting working groups, free meeting

format, collaborative agenda and flexible meeting duration improved our collaboration so much that we extended it from governance and tactical meetings to encompass all company meetings.

The influence of Open Space has helped us self-organise around topics that needed to be discussed and work to be done - all by by contributors who have chosen to do so.

It has played a large part in keeping high levels of engagement in the new way of working: No one felt forced to go to boring meetings or to participate in improvement projects they had little interest in. It helped us amplify our culture of freedom and continuous improvement.

Conclusion

We've seen how powerful a combination of Sociocracy, Holacracy, Agile and Open Space can be to drive continuous improvement, provide clarity and visibility across an organisation, and get decisions made quickly with the right people involved.

For us, the combination has formed a system we employ to support principles and values we agree with, such as distributed leadership, accountability, continuous improvement and transparency.

3.4 The New Synthesis - Self-Organization

A common goal, shared values, and ideals around equivalence in power, mutual respect, and fairness enables all levels of a company to self-organize. Therefore, it is important to take time to build clarity about the common goal and agreements around values.

All the different streams suggest a change in structure to support self-organization and the combination of the streams reinforces this the following way:

- Self-organization is sparked by a common aim, equivalence, or/and shared values. These define the container, thus the aim and value have an impact on the width or narrowness of the container.
  - The container is stronger if the aim is based on the customer's needs because the customer brings in an outside pressure or force that drives the self-organization phenomena.
- Cross-functionality for including all necessary and different perspectives. The variety in perspectives must be balanced with the common aim.
- Trust in the wisdom of the individuals and their interactions, which means fewer rules and guidelines. They become semi-autonomous because they are not micromanaged.

  - Setting up rules and guidelines that assume all employees want to contribute positively to the company's success.
  - Relying on self-selecting teams / groups emphasizes this trust.
- Retrospectives for adapting the process (and structure) for the actual needs.
- Decision-making procedures based on consent for creating equivalence - an equal voice for everyone involved.
- Double-linking for creating a bottom-up link (next to the usual top-down link), which builds a feedback loop in a hierarchy.
- Organize open meetings, where anyone who cares about the issue is invited to attend or even call the meeting, and the topic is the priority. Totally new things can emerge, and the schedule bends to that priority.

Self-organization creates trust. If the structures for encouraging
self-organization are working well, then the level of trust should
build over time.

4. Transparency

By "transparency" we mean making information accessible so that people can make knowledgeable decisions. With all the streams, transparency is necessary for the methods to work. They are intertwined. For example, transparency is necessary for continuous learning and constant customer focus. However, there is a long-standing habit in work cultures of hiding. "Don't tell the employees we're about to have a layoff because we'll lose all our best people." or "I'm trying to accomplish this innovative idea, and I'm going to keep it a secret to keep down the resistance." And so forth. Transparency, in other words, may be uncomfortable as an organization transforms itself company-wide. In the end it may be a relief to be freed from the draining burden of maintaining secrets.

4.1 Challenges with Implementing Transparency

Transparency isn't easy. If a team has a customer that has a hidden use for the product, the team will fail to deliver what the customer really needs. If there is a management power fight going on that involves manipulation, the team won't be able to get all the information it needs to deliver a usable product. Moreover, there often is a lot of information that can create an information overload and a huge burden on everybody to filter.

Transparency is essential for success. It is not just about sharing information but about structuring in a way that makes that sharing possible in an effective way. If you don't have people who know what information is lacking, the team will never be able to understand the whole problem at hand. Some time ago, experiments with total quality management stopped because they led to deep frustration and resentment. Teams would work on a project for months only to have management reject their work because it didn't really meet their needs. Understanding the whole picture requires us to structure a process in which management is involved.

To paraphrase Michael Herman: troubles can be "bounded by transparency." (see Herman). Transparency is a trouble detector, because when you implement it, existing problems (often long existing) can no longer be hidden. Thus, transparency is a key to finally solving these problems. But, what if the existing company culture likes to hide problems?

4.2 Perspectives from the Different Streams

The four streams have interesting differences in the way they approach transparency.

Beyond Budgeting

Beyond Budgeting leadership principle 3 says "make information open for self-regulation, innovation, learning and control and **don't** restrict it." Transparency is - according to one of the co-founders of Beyond Budgeting, Jeremy Hope - "the new control system." Thus, a group can only make an informed decision if the information is actually available to them. Yet, making information available also creates more vulnerability and even fear because there is no way to hide bad news. This vulnerability results in a different kind of control, control through timely access to reality and opportunities for creativity around any observed problems. In other words, transparency creates self-regulation through social pressure.

Open Space

Open Space builds on transparency by ensuring all topics that need to be discussed are on the table and are not dealt with in a hidden room. Moreover, it asks not to wait for the "right" people to show up to discuss a specific topic but rather to trust that whoever joins the discussion are the right people. They are the ones who cared enough to show up and do the work on the topic. Transparency does not mean everyone receives all information but people who need the information will seek it and be able to get it. People who are seeking for information will get the information.

Thanks to Michael Herman who pointed us to a great ongoing Organizational Open Space example from the University of Kentucky Center for Rural Health (see Kepferle & Main):

There are only five constraints on this model of personal empowerment:

1. When a problem or opportunity is to be discussed, there must be wide notification of the meeting time and place so anyone who is interested can attend.
2. Proposed solutions/ideas must be broadcast widely so they can be acknowledged as Center policies, programs or procedures; or, if they are contradictory to University of Kentucky rules, another solution can be sought.
3. Proposed solutions cannot be hurtful to anyone else.
4. Proposed solutions should channel our limited resources in such a way as to have maximum impact on achieving our goal.
5. Accomplishing the work for which we were hired takes precedence over our group work. However,

if the RIGHT people (those who really care) are involved in any topic, they will find a way to make sure their work is completed and the work of the group is brought to a successful conclusion.

There are NO CONSTRAINTS on the following:

1. Who can call a meeting.
2. The type of problem or opportunity that is being addressed.
3. The availability of time to have a meeting.
4. Who may attend a meeting.
5. The availability of information necessary for a group to work.

The rules mean everyone can see what everyone else cares about and is taking responsibility for. Relying on invitations over mandates and assignments makes the illusion of control transparent. Because any issue or opportunity of importance can be raised in Open Space, it brings a level of transparency to the environment and to what is happening. The right and responsibility to invite, to call a large meeting, or convene a breakout session within a meeting is equivalent to the right and responsibility to "pull the cord" in a Toyota factory plant.

Sociocracy

Sociocracy defines transparency as access to all the information you need to make a decision - not as everyone can see all the information. Everyone must be able to see all the information they need. It means there are no insurmountable barriers to getting the information a team needs to make its decisions. Someone who hides information can manipulate and control others, and that violates the need for equivalence, discussed under self-organization.

When a team makes a joint decision, it starts with "picture-form-ing," which means gathering all the information relevant to an issue before it starts developing solutions. At this stage, it may need to ask difficult ("sticky") questions and it will need answers. For example, a company might require its accounting department to shield the company's financial overhead so that competitors don't gain an advantage when calculating their bid rates on contracts. But, a sociocratic team (also known as "circle") may want to know if its profit sharing payments are being calculated correctly. One way to resolve these conflicting needs is for the circle to select a representative acceptable to both the team and the accounting department to examine and validate the accuracy of the books.

Agile

Agile makes both the work and the process for creating the work transparent. Transparency is what's really going on. Thus, a team deliberates jointly with the customer what it will work on next and how achieving its deliverable can be measured. While creating the work, the team makes the progress transparent e.g. in Scrum by presenting the working software at the review meeting to the stakeholder. The actual and regular delivery of the system is key to transparency, because everyone who is interested in the team's work can tell exactly what and how much has been completed. In contrast, with non-agile teams the information about progress often can't be found or verified because there is only documentation and no executable system to provide this information. While the documentation may provide lots of information, that really doesn't mean much because only the product at the end is verifiable, which everyone hopes will be usable.

In contrast, with non-agile teams the information about progress often can't be found or verified, because there is no executable system to provide this information - only documentation that may provide lots of information that really doesn't mean much because only the product at the end is verifiable, which everyone hopes will be usable.

4.3 The New Synthesis - Transparency

The surprising conclusion is that the four streams are very consistent in the way they define transparency. A composite definition might be: *transparency is a structure that reliably shows the truth to those who need to know it.* Transparency doesn't mean that information can't be managed to meet legally required confidentiality and information overload. Each stream recommends specific structural disciplines that - combined - help everyone know the truth, including:

- Make your work and the progress toward the result transparent.
    - It is often uncomfortable information, yet if you don't know about it you can't act on it.
    - Information is based on verifiable facts (like a concrete delivery).
- Make information available and accessible to the people who need it to do their work.
    - Picture forming is used to gather relevant information before developing solutions.
    - All necessary information is shared.
    - Self-organizing teams have all the information needed to deliberate a topic.

5. Constant Customer Focus

By "constant customer focus" we mean the alignment of the interests of both the customer and the company providing the service or product. Customers are typically the persons or institutions who receive products or services from the company. However, they can be any entity with whom you interface, for example, shareholders or regulatory agencies. Sometimes customers' needs might be in conflict, for example, serving the Mafia (as a possible customer) would contradict legal regulations. Thus, customer focus needs to be balanced.

You might argue that constant customer focus is the driver for all other values because external customer focus seems to be the underlying value for being an agile company. When you ask "why," customer focus is always the answer. For example, if we ask, "why is self-organization important?" or "why do we need transparency or to learn continuously?" the answer is because we want to serve our customer. Yet, the company itself is also a customer. It must survive and thrive without saying that the company's main business is to make money (see Leybourn.) So, you can also answer this "why" question about values with the answer "the company needs to survive and thrive." So there is a paradox: there are actually two customers - the company itself and external customers. The trick is to synthesize the interests of both kinds of customer using a win-win approach.

The quote by Jeremy Hope et al that begins this Part provides a great example for such a win-win approach. The sentiment expressed in the quotation ends up treating shareholders, external customers, and employees as "first" because the needs of all parties are met. We particularly look at sociocracy to resolve this conundrum.

The other word in the value of constant customer focus is "constant." In a traditional factory, the customer places an order and receives a product at the end of the production process. The constant customer focus value calls for joint learning that leads to a tight relationship with the customer during the whole process, regardless of the nature of the product - or service. This relationship goes both ways. On the one hand, the customer receives frequent and regular deliveries (product increments). On the other hand the customer provides frequent and regular feedback, which steers the production into the right direction so that the product serves the customer's needs. For example, a shoe manufacturer enables customers to design their own shoes online. A school in a university involves students in the running of the school as well as industry representatives. A bakery invites customers to special order new kinds of pastry. And "of course" in software development the system is explored together with the client to find out jointly how it could serve the client best. Before we will look into the details of how all the different streams approach constant customer focus, we explore some of the challenges.

5.1 Challenges with Establishing Company-wide Customer Focus

Different than the agile approach, Beyond Budgeting, Open Space, and Sociocracy do not call for a role that ensures customer focus. This role, in Agile named product owner, has proven useful because it assigns specific resources to manage the focus, a focus that may be more diffuse in the other methods. However, the relationship of the product owner role to the rest of the company is often unclear, and there is no clear guidance on how to embed an internal (meaning being an employee of the company) product owner in the organization.

For example, a company might say it has a customer focus and then have annual performance reviews of product owners that contain objectives developed elsewhere in the company that do not attune to what the particular customer actually needs and are too long term. The product owners then can't keep their constant customer focus because then they wouldn't get their bonus. To avoid this outcome, agile teams rely on product owner heroism. A better strategy is to create a structure that eliminates the problem.

Another example: the internal product owner is ensuring that the team has a constant customer focus, and then someone from elsewhere in the company suddenly pops up, asserts authority, and undermines that customer focus. A product owner can avoid this danger by including such potential disruptors in the stakeholder collaboration process so that their concerns can be taken into account along with other perspectives. Again, however, a company-wide structure would eliminate the need for a product owner to be a "clever political tactician."

A key question, then, is can we preserve the valuable aspects of the product owner function and use methods from the other three streams to overcome the inherent challenges?

5.2 Perspectives from the Different Streams

We turn to the other streams for insights into how to embed the product owner function in the company's structure so that a constant customer focus is built-in. Sociocracy, for example, has some unique contributions to the question of customer focus and the role of shareholders. We then turn to Agile to explore the rich set of agile customer-focus tools that have developed in part because of the existence of an explicit product owner role.

Beyond Budgeting

Beyond Budgeting recognizes three separate budget purposes and treats them separately:

- Target setting: A *target* is what we want to happen, reflecting our ambitions.
- Forecasting: A *forecast* is what we think will happen, whether we like what we see or not.
- Resource allocation: *Resource allocation* is about what it takes to make it happen, it is about optimizing scarce resources.

In a conventional budget, these three different purposes are typically addressed in one process which results in one set of numbers: the budget. However, this approach often creates conflicts. For example, when people are asked to make a sales forecast, they often reduce their forecasts to make sure the final number is something they know they will hit or exceed. Another example is a cost forecast that a line manager makes who also knows it is the only chance for getting access to resources for next year. We all know what happens: gaming, sandbagging, lowballing and, of course, biased forecasts as discussed in Chapter 2.

Such conflicts can be solved by separating the three purposes into three different processes, allowing each one to operate with different numbers and be executed in different ways. The following list explores these concepts further:

- Relative targets: should reflect our ambitions but when possible avoid absolute targets; instead the targets should relate to competitors' performance or others we can compare ourselves with. Bjarte Bogsnes, chairman of the Beyond Budgeting Institute, details, "The purpose of such targets should, however, mainly be learning (especially internally), with the gentle performance push as a nice side effect. Nobody likes to be laggards. It can also be about rounded and mid-term ambition levels, sometimes expressed as a range etc. Some organizations go further and skip targets. They find other ways of setting ambition levels and evaluating performance."

- Rolling forecasting: this strategy is a way to improve forecasting by estimating what lies ahead and what needs to be adjusted. To do a rolling forecast, we ask frequently, how are we doing, how are market conditions, and where are they likely to head? What are the implications for us? As Bjarte Bogsnes reports from his experience: "A rolling forecast is typically updated every quarter, always looking for instance five quarters ahead. Some, like Norwegian Statoil, go for a more event-driven *dynamic forecasting*, with no predefined frequency or time horizon. The line updates their own forecasts when something happens which they believe justifies a forecast update. With a shared forecasting database, anyone can tap into the latest updated information when needed."
  - Note: a rolling forecast is not a "rolling budget" also serving the two other budget purposes, target setting and resource allocation, These are handled in separate processes as described above and below.
- Dynamic resource allocation: means "continuous delivery" of resources. Bjarte Bogsnes elaborates, "The key is to avoid the annual, detailed budget pre-allocation of resourcesbecause the annual budget is a 'too big batch' of decisions. Instead, a more continuous delivery is applied, where decisions are made *at the right time and at the right level.* This means as late as possible, securing better information not just about the project or activity to be decided, but also about the capacity to execute. This information comes from the latest forecasts available. "At the right level" means as far out in the organization as possible. For operating costs with less distinct decisions points, a number of alternative cost management tools can be used, from an overall 'burn rate guiding' to unit

cost targets, or only monitoring of actual costs trends with interventions when needed only."

The target, forecast, and resource allocation are all tightly tied into the customer relationship. They enable what we are producing for the customer and how fast we are providing the product or service. Hence, the question of "what serves the customers best" is always at the core because what is good for the customer is good for the company.

Beyond Budgeting also makes it very clear that teams' or individuals' performance evaluations have an impact on the customer focus. Performance evaluation must, for instance, take into account the market conditions and changes such as customer priorities or competing products. That is why objectives, if possible, are set relative to the market, to a different team, or to one's own performance and not fixed for a long period of time, ignoring changing conditions. This approach addresses the potential conflict, mentioned above, in which an individual's objectives contradict actual customer needs. As Bjarte Bogsnes comments, "A holistic performance evaluation is key in Beyond Budgeting. 'Not everything that counts can be counted and not everything that can be counted counts.' The less relative targets are, the more it is needed. The purpose is to reflect hindsight insights; headwind or tailwind, ambition levels set, risks taken and sustainability of results."

Performance measurement can be based on KPIs. The "I" in KPI stands for indicator and seldom tells the full truth (see Bogsnes 2017). As Bjarte Bogsnes emphasizes: "They are not called KPTs, Key Performance Truth!" We have to look behind the indications before we can really judge actual performance. Performance evaluation should not be about individual incentives because learning is more significant - especially for the whole company's success.

Beyond Budgeting reflects the extensive research that shows purpose, mastery, autonomy, and belonging are much more effective motivators than money when it comes to knowledge work. Furthermore, Beyond Budgeting recognizes that today's work can hardly be individualized because it is typically a team effort. Individual incentives are, therefore, not recommended as they often drive suboptimal behaviors. Common bonus schemes driven by shared success should be used instead.

Finally, the late Jeremy Hope, one of the thought leaders of Beyond Budgeting, explored the structural concept that the whole focus of the company should shift from cost and profit to a focus on the value being delivered to the customer. This shift leads to restructuring the whole company so that instead of cost- and profit-centers there are only value centers and support service teams such as Finance and Marketing (see Hope). The support service teams don't control the value centers but rather collaborate with them. The focus is on the value centers where the value for the customer is created. For example, Swedish Handelsbanken trusts every branch to service their market in their own way. The only central expectation is for branches to judge what is best for the customer.

Open Space

Periodic Open Space gatherings can support Agile, Beyond Budgeting, and Sociocracy during their times of review and adjustment in focusing on the customer. Moreover, the topics worked on in Open Space meetings often focus on the customer. Yet, customer focus is not a prerequisite; Open Space used only as a facilitation technique does not offer specific guidance for ensuring constant customer focus.

However, some companies such as Valve Corporation are using Open Space to organize themselves (see Valve). Used in this way, Open Space makes a unique and significant contribution: Passion. It is common to hear a manager wonder, "How we can get the same enthusiasm for the company's work that we see in voluntary projects?" Without Open Space such managers might actually be seeking enthusiasm for their own ideas. Yet, as a manager, you do not need to worry about enthusiasm because people naturally care about their work having value and meaning. Open Space lets them pursue that directly as a team.

You see this passion, bounded by responsibility, in a similar approach called Open Source. For example, when Linus Thorvald decided he wanted a better operating system, he started developing Linux and announced that he was doing so. Many others volunteered to help. In general, in a company using Open Space, if an employee discovers an unmet customer need, she goes back to the company and proposes to address that need - and if enough people want to work on it, they will organize to provide the corresponding product or service. She doesn't need to get permission first.

Another way of ensuring constant customer focus with organizational Open Space is by inviting the customers to collaborate on designing new products. Thus, Open Space offers a unique way to combine customer focus, emergence of new ideas, and passion bounded by responsibility.

Sociocracy

As with Agile and Beyond Budgeting, Sociocracy emphasizes customer focus. It treats customer focus as a systems matter and its abstract formulation helps apply the concept company-wide. Its formulation is helpful in addressing the apparent conflict between shareholders and customer focus noted in Chapter 1.

Common Aim

Sociocracy asserts that "common aim," which incorporates customer focus, is the force that brings a team together and induces it to organize. An aim is "a product or service, differentiated from other products or services, that the customer understands and desires. It is the basis for exchange with the customer." The team outputs products or services to the customer and in exchange gets feedback from the customer in the form of money, other products and services, and/or non-quantitative expressions of acceptance.

The "aim" is the team's output desired by its customer and from this output we can reverse engineer the sales, production, and delivery processes needed to create the output. The following diagrams illustrate this concept and are, incidentally, closely related to the formulation laid out in the ISO-9000 Quality Standard (see ISO9000).

Linear "Doing" Process: From Marketing to Production to Delivery/Customer Acceptance

To this linear process we add (a) closed feedback loops for process control and (b) an open feedback relationship with the customer. This pattern in Sociocracy is, underneath the different terminology typically used in agile methods, the same fundamental pattern. The key is being very clear that you must make every effort to not only get customer feedback but also by anticipating the evolution or even revolutions in customer needs.

Feedback is a flow of information back to its origin, a circular causal process in which a system's output is returned to its input, possibly involving other systems in the loop (see Krippendorff). For readability, Sociocracy translates "input", "other system," and "output" into "Lead, Do, Measure." There are many different terminology conventions for describing feedback loops. For example, the Deming-cycle is "Plan, Do, Check, Act" and the agile version calls for "Plan, Do, Inspect, Adapt". The agile version incorporates learning into the cycle through the work "inspect." Sociocracy incorporates learning into a separate but related process called "development," the process of a systematic unfolding of a system's structure (see again Krippendorff).

Feedback is a fundamental pattern. It means that for every step in your production process there should be a guiding loop that leads by developing formal or informal policies, procedures, and work instructions and also measures the effectiveness of those policies and procedures. When such loops are in place stability and high quality result. For example, this diagram summarizes the concepts of the International quality standard, ISO 9000 (see ISO 9000).

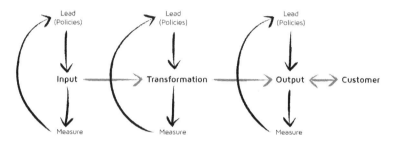

Linear Doing Process Guided By Feedback Loops

In this diagram the arrows demonstrate that the measured results are considered and not ignored by those leading. They then make adjustments based on the measurements.

Relationship with Owners

If we extend this diagram one step further on a company-wide basis, we see that we must treat the shareholders as one of many equivalent voices in control of the company. To establish this equivalence, Sociocracy treats investment money contributed by the shareholder/investors as condensed labor. This concept is helpful in calculating the shareholder and employees' fair shares of receiving the measurement that is the gains and loss in money. Everyone in the system is both worker and entrepreneur. Further, because the shareholders are included in a feedback loop, they must pay attention to feedback. Feedback does not work if you listen to it sometimes and not others. Shareholders becoming part of the feedback means that they consent to joining a system that thinks together. They "rewire" their power to create a system that thinks smarter. Among other services, shareholders play a critical role in ensuring financial viability; they are a clear mechanism that oversees and directs scarce resources.

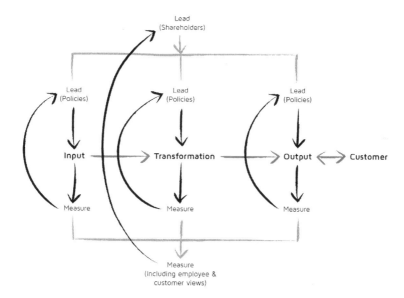

Multi-level Feedback Loops Including Shareholders and Other Stakeholders

The key is being very clear that you must make every effort to not only get customer feedback but to anticipate changes in customer needs. The Sociocracy way to ensure there is a shared focus is to use *double-linking*, discussed above in section Self-Organization. The generalized formulation used by Sociocracy makes it clear that even the shareholders should share this focus. An agile company needs a new style of board and new legal structure and bylaws to support the new configuration (see Buck & Villines). With the whole company organized around customer focus, no one again can suddenly assert authority that undermines the customer focus.

Agile

In Agile there are a number of approaches to establishing customer focus. Close collaboration with and among all the stakeholders, i.e., everyone who has an interest in the product is the core principle. This collaboration is the foundation for setting the priorities on what will be worked on or rather what will be delivered in the next time period, e.g., two weeks. Moreover, after this delivery, the system is reviewed jointly and through this collaboration the customer feedback will make sure that needs have been addressed with the delivery. In addition to these techniques (involving the customer, regular and frequent deliveries and feedback) other practices have been combined with Agile, such as minimum viable product, user stories and personas, value stream analysis (influenced by Lean Startup), and Design Thinking. One example is to use Design Thinking for exploring and solving problems, Lean Startup as the framework for testing beliefs, and Agile for adapting to changing conditions (see Schneider.)

We will now look into these other practices.

Minimum Viable Product influenced by Lean Startup

With Agile the development approach changes completely. Whereas in a linear - often called waterfall approach - the focus is typically on achieving the milestones, in Agile it is on meeting customers' needs. For example, in a waterfall software project the team would first work on analyzing all requirements, which means for a long time nothing can be presented to the customer and therefore it is hard to receive any valuable feedback. An agile project, however, is based on getting and incorporating feedback, so the process is "nonlinear." The team delivers value to the customer fast and frequently to obtain that feedback and learn. Frequent delivery means an agile team starts building a tiny slice of the whole system, which still provides a value for the customers and so they can provide feedback early on. From the Lean Startup approach this tiny slice is called the minimum viable product (MVP), which is the smallest product one can think of and which is discussed with the customer for feedback (see Ries). Subsequently this slice will be broadened till the system is covering everything that is needed by the customer.

User Stories and Personas

In a waterfall project the requirements would be expressed in an almost technical way ensuring the different states of the system are well articulated. In Agile however, requirements are expressed as user stories, which are scenarios covering how a user will work with the system. This approach is based on the insight that narratives are much richer than formal requirements and thus better in conveying what is requested by the customer.

To cover the needs of different users, the team, Product Owner, and user research specialists create so-called personas (more about personas below in Design Thinking), each representing a very specific user. The personas are then used for creating user stories.

Value Stream Analysis influenced by Lean Development

In order to focus on the customer, the whole organization has to have a clear picture about how value for the customer is actually created. This means across teams, departments, roles, and hierarchies there should be a clear understanding about what kind of actions, processes, and collaborations support or hinder value creation. A most helpful tool for achieving this clear understanding is a value stream analysis, which means the creation of a streamline visualizing what is happening inside the company from the first idea supporting the customer (this can be also triggered by a customer request) till the actual delivery is in the customer's hands. The following diagram depicts a typical value stream for a company receiving a customer request. It is applicable to all kinds of customer requests.

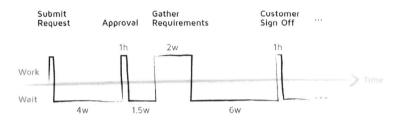

Example Value Stream Analysis

The streamline shows times people work on a request and times nothing is happening with a request, so-called waiting time. Using a value stream analysis gives the company an understanding of how a value for the customer is actually created. Such a value stream analysis also makes transparent where costs of delay are created and thus need to be reduced for keeping an improved focus on the customer (see Reinertsen and Rothman & Eckstein). So the value stream analysis shows where and when no value is created but time is wasted. Thus, if a company wants to focus on the customer, it needs first to create an understanding about the cost of delay visualized by the value stream analysis and then look for ways to eliminate the waiting time to speed up the working time.

Design Thinking

Design Thinking is based on frequent interactions with the end user - especially via feedback and interviews - for learning more about specific preferences, experiences, and emotions. The whole process focuses on "personas", concrete user models with concrete characteristics and behaviors, which help to understand how the new idea will improve the life of this end user. To develop a complete understanding about the needs and motivation of these personas, a multidisciplinary team brings different perspectives to all steps in the Design Thinking process. These steps are shown in the figure below.[1]

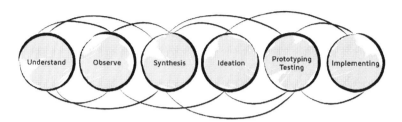

The Design Thinking Process

As can be seen in the figure above, the process is iterative; thus, the lines indicate iterative movement in both directions. The steps include:

- Understand - end user's needs and motivation.
- Observe - how the end users are working in the specific field, which might focus on e.g. how they deal with a product or how they provide a service.
- Synthesis - from the multidisciplinary perspectives (of understanding and observing) create a shared understanding by the cross-functional design team.
- Ideation - Use the synthesis developed in the step before for creating different ideas that have a chance of improving the end users' lives.
- Prototyping / Testing - test the ideas (which is comparable to an MVP - minimum viable product).
- Implement - Put into production the ideas that pass the tests successfully.

The iteration is deep. For example, even after a late step like proto-typing, more can be learned about the user's needs by observation, which might then change the whole idea.

5.3 The New Synthesis - Constant Customer Focus

We explored three ways (value stream analysis, Sociocracy work-flow, and Design Thinking process) of depicting the workflow process. The workflow depends on a system of feedback loops that enable constant customer focus by continually adapting to customer needs. It seems worthwhile to use each depiction to analyze your organization to ensure that you are highly attuned to your customer. Each depiction must describe the fundamental pattern of production. The language used to articulate this pattern needs to be adapted to the individual circumstances of the organization and its customers. Agile, Sociocracy, and Design Thinking offer three different vocabularies. It is important to be aware of the underlying patterns and not identify them with a particular vocabulary.

However, all streams say:

> "Organize to serve your customer. Organize each facet of the company around coordinating services offered to any one customer. The kind of work and the customer's convenience should drive the review and real-location of resources, not the calendar."

Each stream contributes a different insight, which combined, creates the following synthesis:

- Ensure that the customer focus is the aim, the reason for people working together as a team

- Use a cross-functional team so that the customer focus is understood from all angles (different perspectives).
- Allow the people working together to follow their passion for doing work that matters and delights their customers. Thus, they organize to honor passion bounded by responsibility.

- Establish a bidirectional relationship with your customer. **Ensure that the customer can learn from the deliveries** and that the company can learn from the customer - both throughout the production process.
  - Observe and understand the end users' needs. Use the concept of personas for ensuring this understanding.
  - Build scenarios, or rather user stories to comprehend how the product or service will help solve the end users' problems.
  - Use an MVP, a minimum viable product, for testing the waters.
  - Be sure to get early and frequent feedback from your customer in order to build the right thing, which means iterate, iterate, and iterate again.
  - Consider establishing a Product Owner function to maintain the bidirectional relationship.

- Ensure your budgeting approach is flexible toward customer and market needs. Do not fix the budget long-term upfront; make budgeting fit the customer focus.
  - Eliminate time wasted by deleting (or at least reducing) the activities and processes that are not focusing on the customer as uncovered by a value stream analysis. Thus, don't make the customer wait.
  - Have performance reviews, individual goals, and incentives aligned with the customer focus, including board members and the board team. The process is to hold performance reviews where the goals and incentives focus on the customer.

- Enable the board of directors to be open to feedback from and measurement by the customer
    - The structure is to have representatives from the staff serve a full members on the Board (double-link representative) - as well as outside representatives who have different perspectives on the customer.
    - A process is to include customer feedback in each board meeting.
    - Establish multi-stakeholder control of the company. Address this fundamental issue by providing a specific legal structure to establish the multi-stakeholder environment.
    - Departments that provide support to the departments that directly serve the customer should collaborate and not control each other.

6. Continuous Learning

The originator of retrospectives, Norm Kerth clarified that (see Kerth, 2001, p. 5):

> "[r]etrospective rituals are more than just a review of the past. They also provide a chance to look forward, to plot the next project, and to plan explicitly what will be approached differently next time." – Norm Kerth

By "continuous learning" we mean the constant growth of personal and collective skills, abilities, and knowledge through, for example: inspecting, experimenting, teaching, giving and getting feedback, reflection, working on the job, collaboration, reading, training, and assembled instruction.

In Chapter 2 we said that an organization needs regular feedback for enabling continuous learning by everyone. In the established agile methods, a team finds out in a retrospective what it needs to learn by looking back at its performance to date as well as looking forward to anticipate what it needs to do next to serve its customer. From either view, it gets information that says, "organize a learning and development process in the following ways...." Thus, for example, establishing regular retrospectives not only at the team level but also both within and across all hierarchy levels and roles provides the basis for organizational learning and development. So this way a retrospective helps a company learn from their way of working and make adjustments in order to thrive.

6.1 Challenges for Continuous Learning

The idea of continuous learning, although noble, is easily forgotten. When companies come under stress, there is always a temptation to reduce the budget for learning - "Cancel that course so and so was going to attend because we need to meet payroll." This viewpoint clearly views learning as a lower priority than other considerations. And, it equates learning with just going to courses! Also, when stress happens, one of the first activities cut may be holding retrospectives.

The Agile Fluency Model builds on exactly what is happening under pressure (see AgileFluency). Thus, according to the model you are only fluent if you adhere to your principles even under stress, e.g., a team that is fluent in Focus on Value will keep doing retrospectives even if it is under pressure. Thus, canceling retrospectives because of stress or changing priorities means that the team (or company) isn't fluent in focusing on value. Something similar happens if a team only focuses on creating new features, which means there is no time for refactoring. Refactoring basically means "cleaning up" the system and ensuring that it still allows to add new features quickly. So, by concentrating only on adding new features and ignoring refactoring, teams lose the possibility of adding the new features, which means the learning that happens over time isn't fed back into the system (as it would with refactoring).

In his book *Exponential Organizations* Salim Ismael and colleagues point out that today for a company to succeed, the rate of learning is more important than the return on investment because the rate of learning provides that return (see Ismael et.al.). Moreover, according to these authors, employees experience the high rate of learning as high compensation.

Early in the use of Agile many groups started using the idea of a "gold card" (see GoldCard). If a software team member took the gold card off of the sprint backlog, the team member was announcing that they were temporarily doing research and not directly working on the sprint goals. Taking the gold card obligates the holder to report back on what they learned. Yet, our experience is that today many are unaware of this tool. They may have the impression that Agile prevents innovation by always focusing everyone on the goal, leaving no space for innovation. The concept of the gold card has many names and variations. For example, Google used the term 20% rule, meaning that employees could use 20% of their time each week for exploring new ideas.

Similarly, the Sociocracy literature recognizes the concept of "development," meaning learning, teaching, and researching in interaction with the aim. Some sociocratic organizations try to reserve at least 5% of work time for development. Again, however, there is often not an established practice that successfully resists the temptation to subordinate development to intense focus on present activities during crises. Yet, doing research during a crisis can be critical. For example, a small plastics company during the recent deep recession found ways to reduce its scrappage rate at the same time it was reducing its workforce. The resulting ability to reduce prices was a critical factor in its survival.

6.2 Perspectives from the Different Streams

All four streams emphasize continuous learning, albeit from different perspectives. We call on other perspectives in this section, including Lean Start-up, Human Systems Dynamics, scientific method, quest for professionalism, and adult learning.

Beyond Budgeting

"Principle 11: Performance evaluation - Evaluate performance holistically and with peer feedback for learning and development; not

based on measurement only and not for rewards only." Often performance evaluation is a kind of judgment; now Beyond Budgeting asks to make this an opportunity to learn jointly. Thus, rather than a supervisor judging the behavior and results of an employee, he or she organizes the feedback from colleagues to help the employee improve. Moreover, this feedback is meant to look at all contributions this employee makes to the company and not only on a subset that has been defined in the individual objectives beforehand. Today, people don't solve problems by themselves but instead rely on collaboration. Therefore, the performance evaluation has to take into account both seeking and giving peer support.

Additionally Beyond Budgeting suggests separating the bonus from individual objectives. The reason is that today there is hardly any kind of work that can be done by a person solely. Almost every kind of work requires collaboration with others. Therefore, there is no single achievement and thus also no individual bonus.

Open Space

The law of mobility means whenever you realize you aren't learning or contributing (to the learning of others) you should go to a different place where you can to maximize your own learning and contribution. For a company that uses organizational Open Space this law might have the consequence that products will not be created (or projects will not be started) if there isn't a single person who feels that she can learn anything and neither can she contribute to the learning of others by creating that product (or starting that project).

Open Space invites people to invest their time, attention, energy where they sense it will create the greatest return for themselves, the company, and the customers. This invitation generates a tremendous amount of information, experience, skills, ideas, that can be shared with much lower transaction costs than in traditional organizations: more flow and learning. Participants constantly check their internal experience, what's coming up next, and what is happening in groups - all constantly changing. Learning is sometimes messy and painful, especially when it reveals conflicts between or within people's views. Open Space literally gives people room to move, especially in and out of groups that might be taking on challenging or provocative issues. The novel environment and high information content heightens awareness, which is a good start for any kind of learning. As Michael Herman reports from his experience: "I ask a question trying to learn, spark a new conversation, and in the end someone thanks me for my contribution that moved the work forward."

Sociocracy

Development = learning (training), teaching, researching in interaction with your aim. The "learning organization" is a common phrase, but it is a partial strategy. It seems to imply that the company can stay up with rapidly changing times by simply sending employees to workshops and academic courses. Rather, they should develop skills and new solutions by interacting with their environment, not just by absorbing new information. It is a common experience to learn a subject better by trying to teach it. As people advance from apprentice to journeyman to master, regardless of the subject, they are likely to spend more of their training time advancing their skills and knowledge through research than by receiving instruction. This approach is comparable to the pedagogical patterns *Own Words* and *Try it Yourself* where the learner is asked to explore instructional content by teaching it and by experimenting with it (see Pedagogical Patterns).

Development can wander in many directions, and the phrase "in interaction with your aim" gives development a focus. The "aim" is by definition something that the customer understands and finds attractive. Thus, the customer becomes a filter, or touchstone, for what should receive priority in the development process.

Agile

"Responding to change over following a plan". Thus, it is more important to learn and incorporate that learning than to stick to a plan that has been created before the learning happened. This also includes being open to failures. Failures are regarded as learning opportunities and not as malfunctions. Thus, the goal is not to make it right the first time because this goal prevents learning. So, the goal is rather to make it right through incremental learning as a team and together with your customer. This behavior is reinforced if also managers make their failures and respective learning transparent.

Moreover, the last of the twelve agile principles emphasizes: "At regular intervals, the team reflects on how to become more effective then tunes and adjusts its behavior accordingly." (see AgileManifesto). This principle is the foundation for retrospectives - by reflecting on what's helping and what's hindering, the team gets a better understanding about what needs to be changed so that it can serve the customer effectively. The reflection is typically based on the outcome - so what the team did or did not deliver - and on process, so how did the process help or hinder creating the outcome.

6.3 Additional Perspectives

Learning is a very complex phenomenon. The following short synopsis give a flavor of the variety of concepts, reflecting the depth of complexity.

- **Lean Startup** suggests that the research aspect of learning is a highly disciplined process. That implies all the methods of science are in place with some emphasis on publication and exploration of theory and concept. For example, careful formulation of exactly what ideas to build in order to test them in the market, then measure the experience and finally learn from the measurement leads to developing new ideas to build for testing. This approach defines a cycle of experimenting around an hypothesis, and testing this assumption, which kicks off the next hypothesis and helps you come up with innovative ideas all the time rather than just improving what you have. This "pivoting" is a "structured course correction designed to test a new fundamental hypothesis about the product, strategy, and engine of growth." (see Ries)

- **Human Systems Dynamics** echoes this with its *Adaptive Action* approach (see Eoyang & Holladay). As we explained in Chapter 2, Adaptive Action first asks the question 'what' - is the situation at hand, then 'so what' - can we learn from this and what are our insights. And finally 'now what' - is the next step or action we want to take which after execution will lead to the next cycle, meaning asking again 'what'. This compares to the Lean Startup cycle of build (now what) - measure (what) - learn (so what). You can start anywhere, the important thing is that it really is a cycle which is closed, so the learning can always go on.

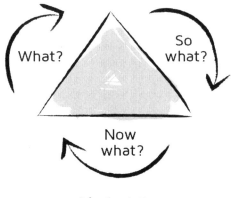

Adaptive Action

- The **scientific method** is an important guide to research (see Garland).
  - Define a question.
  - Gather information and resources (observe).
  - Form an explanatory hypothesis.
  - Test the hypothesis by performing an experiment and collecting data in a reproducible manner.
  - Analyze the data.
  - Interpret the data and draw conclusions that serve as a starting point for new hypothesis, i.e., loop back to an earlier part of the process.
  - At the same time, publish results followed by a retest (frequently done by other scientists).

  It is one thing to do experimentation using, e.g., Lean Startup, but are you also publishing your results for peer review? We often encourage our clients to present at conferences, write experience reports, or other articles which helps them to understand what has happened, what they did and what the consequences were. Coming up with a presentation or writing about it helps people reflect on their learning - and is also a reward. It emphasizes how important it is to socialize with your peers by replicating it with them and in this way validating your learning.

- **Quest for Professionalism**: building on these thoughts about scientific method, Romme points out that there is a long term disconnect between academics and business (see Romme). Romme argues that lawyers or doctors need to have a licence to work in their profession and although leadership is in many cases as important (and can do as much harm) there is no objective assurance that a person in a leadership position knows what she is doing. Unlike other professional areas, academic institutions do not particularly contribute to companies' Lean Startup type research. In the long run, it would be good to repair this gap. Romme points out that if we had empirically validated management practices, we would have the basis for licensing managers.

- **Adult Learning**: Adult learning theorists assert that effective leaders lead through learning (see Drago-Severson et.al). The leaders bring adults together as teams that support learning. They don't simply assign or delegate tasks but offer appropriate support and provide growth challenges. They promote collegial inquiry that involves reflecting on one's assumptions, values, beliefs, and commitments. They mentor.

As also articulated in the theory of constructivism, adults filter what they encounter through their "meaning-making system," their current way of constructing their worlds. They can experience continuous learning through this system. However, a transformative learning occurs, often after a period of chaos, when there is a qualitative change in this meaning-making system (see Satir et.al.). Usually this change enables a person to take a broader perspective and may change his or her relationship with other people. Transformative learning tends to be discontinuous - a sudden leap in understanding. Thus, a transformative leader helps everyone periodically advance, often through reflection, much faster than they might if they were only learning continuously.

6.4 The New Synthesis - Continuous Learning

In every case you learn through interaction with your environment, a concept perhaps best articulated in the academic literature. What Agile and Sociocracy assert is that the vessel that holds the learning is the customer focus.

By synthesizing different formulations we are better prepared to generalize the continuous learning concept to a company-wide venue. Continuous learning requires structure across different teams, roles, and hierarchies that:

- Follows a regular rhythm which creates space for feedback.
  - Defines an hypothesis first, then experiments around this hypothesis and learns from the results - which then feed into the next hypothesis.
- Focuses on the aim (customer focus) of the company and promotes not just training but also teaching and organized research. Organized research includes sharing or publishing what you are learning with peers so that they can attempt to replicate and validate your conclusions.
  - During performance evaluation relate measurement to customer focus and organize learning and development for the individual so that it supports organizational growth.
  - Separate individual objectives from bonus.
- Stays open to dramatically new learning paths that may emerge spontaneously by interrupting daily routines (e.g., moments of silence in a meeting, retrospectives especially when you are under stress, hold an ad hoc Open Space for new ideas).

- Uses failure as a learning opportunity and makes the learning transparent and independent of the function in the organizational structure.
- Reflect and learn both from outcomes and from interactions.

7. A New Tune

In this concluding chapter for Part II we overview the fusion of the four streams and ask what impact it has. We present a new perspective on the organigram (short for organizational diagram, also known as organizational chart) to illustrate the impact. Then we look at the Titansoft company, an example of combining the streams. Finally, we provide a summary of Part II.

7.1 A New Organigram

In Part II, we encountered several views about control of the company. One perspective said that the board is responsible for the company. Another said the value center is at the core of the company, and the customer is its most dominant influence. A third perspective is that inspiration and passion are really the driver for the company. There is also the idea that the support services teams exert important control as they reflect the legal and resource constraints in which the company operates. There have been attempts in the past to reconcile these different perspectives by depicting organizations as fractal organisms (see Beer, Viable Systems Model). However, what emerged for us was something else. The following is a story of the way the idea of a new organigram developed itself.

Static View

The figure below depicts the classic board perspective of how to organize a company, a logical, top-down, work-breakdown structure that shows the shareholders as ultimately in control. In this static view, the board sits on a "veranda" and surveys its property. Support service teams like finance or HR together with production serve the board. Support service teams help the board regulate production. This static view allows us to draw conclusions about aspects of the dynamics of the organization but doesn't actually depict them.

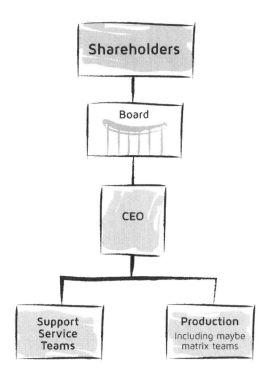

Classic Board Perspective

For example, the figure below includes the dynamics of the board perspective in one area by showing the interaction between production and the external customer. Production seeks feedback from the customer, but often the focus is predominantly on delivering to the customer and less on getting feedback, as reflected by the lighter arrow. The primary measure of success is profit because "profit demonstrates that we are providing what customers want."

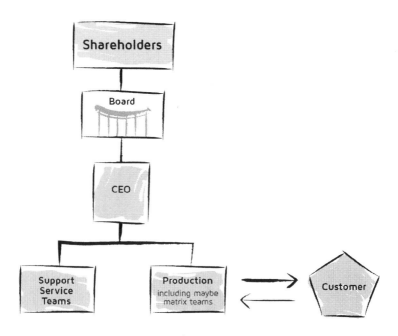

Board Perspective

In our experience, the static organizational chart is misunderstood as depicting both the "work breakdown structure" of the company as well as the dynamic ways it works. This results in employees complaining that "no work would ever get done if we worked only according to the chart." For different processes or procedures people work in complex ways with different people and not necessarily only with the ones they are connected with as shown in the organizational chart. There is still great value in the static depiction because it shows groupings (or containers) of accountabilities, skills, levels of abstraction, and possibly other factors such as geographic distribution. It can be modified to incorporate feedback through double-linking as shown in Chapter 3.

What is needed is differentiated static and dynamic views: - static view of how entities (i.e., business units, departments, teams, individuals, etc.) are grouped with each other; - dynamic view(s) showing how these entities work together depending on the context and request.

Static structures nurture communities, but such structures are per se not alive. Static structures only create the framework for communities. But the community will only come alive with the dynamics. For example, the static placement of houses in a neighborhood may support people in interacting with each other, but unless they actually start talking, a vital neighborhood community won't spring to life.

Dynamic View

There is great value in having a dynamic depiction because we can more easily see complex working relationships, exchanges, and processes. For people working in information technology, it is almost second nature to look at a software program from both static and dynamic perspectives. The static perspective models the entities, data, or classes. In contrast, the dynamic perspective shows the functionality; the processes are visualized typically in a flow chart or a message diagram and are the blueprint for the program or document what is happening in the program. The same logic holds for the "real" world. For example, just because we associate a book with a particular shelf ("all my detective books are on the left side of the upper shelf") doesn't mean that those books always sit on this shelf. You might place a book for several days on your bedside table, lend it to a friend, or put it in your suitcase before a trip. Yet, from a static perspective it still has "its place" on the shelf.

Karen Stephenson has developed the most advanced methodology we are aware of for studying and drawing organization dynamics. She shows the dynamic view of an organization as a trust network[1]. In addition to the static view, Dr. Stephenson uncovers the dynamics and makes them transparent in i.e. career advice networks,

---

[1] https://www.strategy-business.com/article/20964?gko=8942e

social networks, or work networks. The company "community" (or culture) is no longer a mysterious, hard to change phenomenon. With this transparency, culture can change quickly in a supportive way.

In the following figures we explore ways to make the dynamic view more visible.

Value Center Perspective

Referring back to the constant customer focus discussion, the following figure shows cross-functional teams at the core of the company, not the board. In this value center perspective, the customer becomes a kind of leader of the value center, albeit an interactive rather than autocratic one. Note: we use the term "product owner" in the diagram. This term really indicates a function rather than a person. For example, the whole team could decide to handle the function together.

Success means customer satisfaction because a satisfied customer demonstrates that profit is possible and we are providing what the shareholders want - the reverse of the board perspective. Having a force other than the shareholders induces more compelling feedback (i.e., feedback that's harder to ignore) toward the board and support service teams. This change in influence is often experienced as tension, a phenomenon we noted in Chapter 1.

This diagram also recognizes another entity in charge. That entity is society at large, laws, regulations, and agreements with suppliers and contractors that many support service teams represent or give voice to. Bringing in customer focus also induces more feedback to seemingly autocratic regulations.

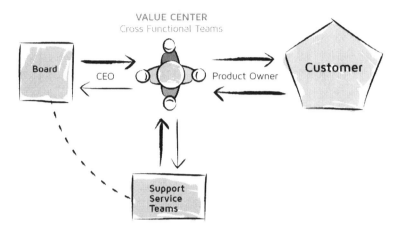

Value Center Perspective

All companies aim to produce value. Conventionally they don't organize around value centers. Instead units that have "a piece of the action" are scattered across silos. This dispersion makes it hard for the value centers to ignite as a unit and really be a effective.

Art and Spirit Perspective

The next view of control introduces a new factor, art and spirit: inspiration, beauty, meaningfulness, self-actualization, and the accompanying passion, which we encountered particularly in our discussion of Open Space Technology. Art and spirit are the foundation of capitalism, not venture capital! The drive to develop new ways to meet needs and express values is the source of the entrepreneurial spirit and the reason new forms and ideas emerge. Inspiration, artistic drive, and passion are the foundation for innovation and continuous learning.

Like other sources of control such as desire for profit and cloying government regulation, art and spirit can also have a downside. For example, the authors have heard staff of a restaurant say, "Food itself and the artistic presentation of food is what drives us; it's nice if our customers like it, but that's not what we most care about." If there is no spirit, the restaurant will soon be a dry shell that crumbles easily and perhaps someone will buy up the pieces. Of course though, too much focus on the intrinsic beauty of a product or service is likely to reduce attention to customer feedback with serious consequences, as reflected by the lighter arrow.

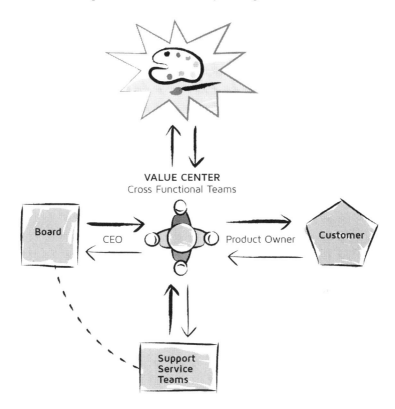

Art and Spirit Perspective

Synthesis of Perspectives

How can we retain the many valuable aspects of the traditional company and also keep the benefits of the value center, inspiration, and legal compliance perspectives? That is, how can we both synthesize and differentiate the various perspectives? The following diagram depicts a BOSSA nova structure that does just that. It shows that there must be collaboration between all the facets of control in a company. For example, support service teams are also connected to art and spirit, because love of beauty or meaningfulness are for them as important as for the value center. We propose to supersede traditional static organigrams with this more multifaceted depiction of power and control in organizations.

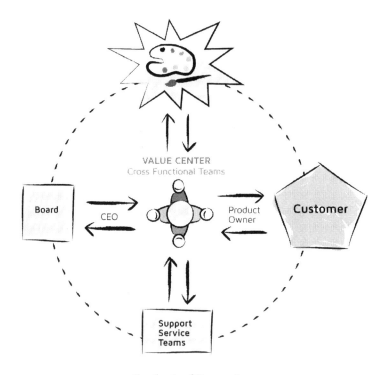

Synthesis of Perspectives

The diagram shows equally prioritized two-way relationships with all aspects of the value center's environment (all strong arrows), a circular power relationship with all four "bosses." These two-way relationships show the implementation of the BOSSA nova in one organigram. It shows the mixing of the streams into one river:

- The two-way relationship between support service teams and production is, in essence, the Beyond Budgeting approach with sociocratic double-linking.
- The two-way relationship between inspiration and the value center is, in essence, the Open Space approach. All four streams of BOSSA nova provide the "feedback to inspiration" as a continuous learning process. An organigram-style drawing would show the visions or muses that inspire the different parts of the company and the learning systems that develop those sensibilities.
- The two-way relationship between the board via the CEO-led management structure and the value center is mediated by strong feedback. This arrangement creates a forum for dialog, as supported by all four streams, between product owners and those in the company who focus on maximizing shareholder value. There is the opportunity for creative resolution of tensions.
- The two-way relationship between value center and customer is, in part, an agile approach generalized beyond a focus on software. Many agile-related tools such as Lean Startup or Design Thinking can help mediate interactions with the customer. However, this relationship is also supported by the concepts of the other streams of BOSSA nova.

The dotted circle indicates that there are also relationships among board, inspiration, customers, and support, each relationship having its own characteristics. It portrays the wholeness that underlies all the systems of specialization. In the whole everyone actually shares ownership for the full value (or damage) delivered by the organization.

We offer this diagram as a comprehensive view of a company. It is fractal in that the four relationships appear at every level of detail. It shows the complexity of both formal structures and informal networks. It captures relationships between different containers (or groupings of similar interests, passion, and responsibilities). We encourage you to experiment with making four-fold drawings at a more detailed level for your specific organization!

Discussion of cross-functional teams

The first two diagrams, above in this chapter, showing the board's perspective, indicates that Production might use "matrix teams."

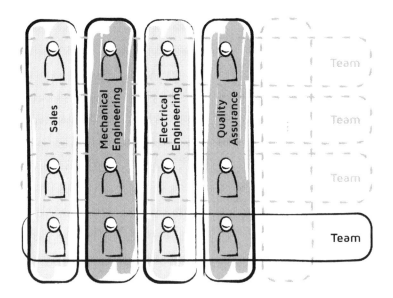

Conventional Cross-functional Team Structure Based on a Matrix

In the board-centered perspective, work is divided into ever smaller units, known as the work breakdown structure. This structure provides the framework for defining roles and writing job descriptions and performance review criteria. A drawback of this approach is that it tends to create "stovepipes," speciality silos that don't communicate effectively. A matrix of teams is a strategy to counteract stovepiping. The vertical columns represent the work breakdown structure. The horizontal rows show dynamic project and product creation by cross-functional teams.

In the value center perspective, self-organizing, cross-functional teams emerge from inspiration and passion to develop an opportunity or to solve a problem, roughly illustrated in the following diagram.

Emergent Cross-functional Team Structure (inspired by AgileLucero)

These two views of cross-functional teams both have value and each has elements of the other. An emergent team, if it is tackling a long-term problem, will likely form an ordered structure. And "rows" in the matrix diagram (e.g., all scrum masters) have the conditions for emergent behavior. The fact that cross-functional teams can be created from top down work-breakdown analysis strategies or just emerge means that they are likely to arise in part from both sources. That means there are many cross-functional strategies, a kind of continuum that can and should be adapted to the needs at hand such as emergent issues, changes, disruptions, opportunities, threats - realities!

7.2 Summary: The Four Values As Instruments in the Band

In Part II we also explored how the four streams support the four values (self-organization, transparency, constant customer focus, continuous learning). Yet, we also looked at how additional concepts, like Lean Startup or Design Thinking contribute to each of the values.

Below find the experience shared by our colleague Yves Lin who combined three of the four values.

Insights from Yves Lin, Titansoft

2014 was the year Titansoft started to adopt Agile and Scrum. The reason back then was simple. We just thought that "Agile is faster". What happened in the next three months after the adoption was unexpected. We started to realize the power of Agile lies in the transparency it creates. We are now able to inspect what we are doing and improve ourselves constantly. We had two product development departments and 5 teams in Singapore then. In terms of organizational structure, we made some changes seeing how Scrum emphasizes self-managing teams. There are no more team leads in teams. No one within teams has authority over other members. The Scrum Master is positioned outside of the team and elected by the team.

Things appeared to be running well. People started to have more communication and share their thoughts more openly. While these were good signs, we also found ourselves facing new problems. What about communication across different teams? Across departments? Beyond physical offices? We started to see long discussions happening within teams. Decisions not being made due to disagreements. Most critically, the organization goal was not being communicated to teams.

We needed a way to create common visions and align goals

across the organization, and learn how to broaden everyone's perspectives and understand each other. Early 2016, we started to find ways to overcome these new challenges. The first few approaches we experimented with were facilitation and Open Space. Learning from the experts, we engaged the Institute of Cultural Affairs (ICA) trainers to conduct ORID (analyze a situation Objective, Reflective, Interpretative, and Decisional) and Consensus workshops and trainings for our senior staff.

Open Space in Titansoft

Our first organization-wide Open Space theme was: "As an organization as well as individuals, what can we do to support each other to grow?" It was a day where the entire company was invited to take a break from work, come together and discuss topics relevant to the theme. Some topics concluded at the end of the day included: training packages for new-comers, what's preventing you from growing as an individual, building vulnerability-based trust in teams and full stack PHP development.

Recognizing the positive feedback from staff about our first Open Space, we decided to plan for our next. Our second company-wide Open Space in the same year was themed around: How can we create the most impact in the next three months? Results from both Open Spaces were evident. We saw members raising varied topics that concerned them, heard differing opinions across roles, and most importantly, employees were given opportunities to listen to diverse perspectives beyond their own. The difficult part emerged after the Open Space happened. How do we sustain momentum for the action topics generated?

Another learning took place, and we decided to try something different again. We hosted our first Participatory Strategic Planning Workshop facilitated by experts from ICA in the same year. A two-day workshop bringing together people across the organization to create strategies for action which will be led by champions to bring back and work on within teams. Through a structured planning process which incorporates consensus building, focused conversations, and an implementation process, we were able to generate a company-wide strategy led by champions in various areas.

Sociocracy in Titansoft

We saw fascinating results from facilitation and Open Space approaches. But problems endured: action and implementation plans still failed to be carried out. Could it be because the action arenas did not fit into teams' daily tasks and there were no official chain of controls from departments to teams? Tasks related to products were accomplished; however, organizational tasks related to recruitment, training and public affairs were easily neglected and left in the dust.

We introduced the sociocracy framework to the organization early 2017 to address these issues, focusing firstly on creating the circle structure and double-linking for more transparent flow of information. The key driving factor behind the adoption was the need to scale effectively. We believe that sociocracy can further strengthen intra-team and inter-team self-organization and communication, and install a communication chain flow from departments to teams, ultimately driving the execution of organizational tasks.

The double-linking model encourages participation in policy decision-making by members of both circles. Each circle has its own focus and in-links can drive team to move forward. The higher circle and top circle is now more aware of what is happening in teams and able to surface problems earlier. Members have clearer channels to give feedback through two-way communication. Policies, strategies and company-wide goals are more easily clarified and circulated among circles, forging stronger alignment together.

Yet, sociocracy is not without its limitations. First and foremost, it is a complex framework consisting of many patterns and principles. Many patterns are easily adopted, but prioritizing which one to work on and mastering the framework is challenging. It is difficult to see how far we can go in adopting

> sociocracy, and success stories are few. The in-links can also easily become the bottleneck for information flow, as they carry more responsibilities including representing decision-making for the team.

Feedback is an essential element underlying all four values. For example,

- Double linking provides the necessary feedback for self-organization to occur company-wide.
- Just by making things transparent you have feedback about what's going on.
- With constant customer focus, by getting early and frequent feedback from your customer you get information that guides you in creating the value that serves the customer's needs and in spending the company's money wisely.
- Feedback appears everywhere in continuous learning from Lean Startup's build, measure, learn, to using retrospectives, to interacting with the environment, to creating new models of reality as articulated in academic literature - all these kinds of learning require feedback.

The following summarizes the BOSSA nova "Value River" that forms from the confluence of the four streams of development.

Self-organization: Use accountable cross-functional teams that select themselves and follow their passion with responsibility.

- Use accountable cross-functional teams
  - At different levels of abstraction
  - With a common aim (meaning clear purpose, measures, and targets) that

  – Govern through shared values and ideals not through rules.
- That
  – Select themselves (for a meaningful duration);
  – Follow their passion with responsibility for whole and meaningful pieces of work;
  – Hold retrospectives and align them across the enterprise to optimize the whole.

Transparency: Create transparency for all involved in two directions by providing information and lowering the barriers to those seeking information:

- Provide information
  – On progress and delivery related to common aim;
- Lower barriers to information needed for
  – Making informed decisions
  – Self-regulation, innovation, and learning.

Constant Customer Focus: "Focus wide" on every aspect of the company: product & process, structure and strategy, and individual contributions and people.

- Product & Process
  – Common aim as, for example, summarized in a minimum viable product;
  – Narratives capturing the ideas of personas in user stories;
  – Feedback on each production step as, for example, made transparent by a value stream analysis.
- Structure & Strategy
  – Includes owners (shareholders),
  – Value centers & support service teams,

- Rolling forecasting.
- Individual contributions / people
  - Passion bounded by responsibility guides contribution,
  - Relative individual objectives not fixed ones.

Continuous Learning: Always learn and contribute to others' learning, get feedback and adapt.

- Always
  - Learning / contributing to others learning guides all work.
- Get Feedback,
  - Retrospectives,
  - Role improvement reviews with peer feedback,
  - Individual objectives separated from bonuses.
- And Adapt
  - Your plans as you develop, where development equals learning (training), teaching, researching in interaction with your aim.

Transparency

Create transparency for all involved in two directions by providing information and lowering the barriers to those seeking information.

Self-organization

Use accountable cross-functional teams that select themselves and follow their passion with responsibility.

Continuous Learning

Always learn and contribute to others' learning, get feedback and adapt.

Constant Customer Focus

"Focus wide" on every aspect of the company: product & process, structure and strategy, and individual contributions and people.

Summary of BOSSA nova "Value River"

In Part III, we address the practical question of how to implement this synthesis (which we've dubbed the BOSSA nova.)

7.3 Final Thought

In general, where does your company stand in terms of the BOSSA nova, the new wave created by the confluence of the four streams? Can you draw a holistic organigram of your company? How well does your company embody the values of company-wide agility?

In Part III we will reflect on strategies, structures, and processes for implementing ("dancing"?) ;-) with the music of Part II.

III Shall We Dance?

"It's not about being able to dance... it's about being willing to dance." – Mary Lynn Manns, Co-Author of Fearless Change

Gain a New Perspective

After we finished Part II, we thought deeply about how to turn the syntheses of the values (self-organization, transparency, constant customer focus, and continuous learning) into a practical tool - the "Now What" question. We reviewed each synthesis and as we reflected noticed that several themes recurred in different values. From these themes patterns emerged. [2] We noted, for example, that feedback pops up repeatedly in the various syntheses. We also noticed a meta pattern by which we could group the themes into:

- Strategy
- Structure
- Process

[2] Patterns defined as a reliable sample of traits, acts, tendencies, or other observable characteristics of a person, group, or institution. For example, a behavior pattern, spending patterns, the prevailing pattern of speech (see Merriam-Webster).

This meta pattern appealed to us because it defines a company (according to Gomez & Zimmermann) from three different perspectives:

- Institutional perspective, which regards a company as a purposeful social system and in this sense a company *is an organization*. The purpose of this social system is guided by the **strategy** of the company.
- Instrumental perspective, which is the **structure** of a company. Or rather: A company *has an organization*, which is understood as its structure.
- Functional perspective, which means to align the activities we do day-to-day. This is expressed in the **processes** of a company. Or, in other words: A company *is being organized*, or rather processed through daily activities.

The following diagram shows the tight relationship between the three perspectives. For example, does strategy follow structure or vice versa?

In summary: a company simultaneously "is an organization", "has an organization," and "is being organized."

You might wonder, where does the company's culture fit in to this meta pattern? Culture is the stories we tell ourselves about ourselves and it is based on purposes, plans, rules, procedures, behaviors, habits etc. These facets very much stabilize the culture. For example, if both teams and the company develop a new habit, the effect can be huge.

Interrelationship of Strategy, Structure, and Process

Corporate culture is defined by the meta pattern of strategy, structure, and processes. So, you change the culture by changing the meta pattern. The strategy, structure, and processes may be that of the conventional hierarchy or they may arise from other hierarchies, e.g., the hierarchy of trust.

Insights from Dr. Karen Stephenson, NetForm International

By pioneering social network analysis at Harvard as a superior means of measuring and managing organizational culture, I demonstrated over decades-long research, that organizational cultures consist of two dynamic interlocking structures: (1) networks of trust and (2) hierarchies of authority. Most people are familiar with hierarchy because they have to learn their place in it when they go to school or get a job. But the real truth is that hierarchy is merely a scaffolding that surrounds a core infrastructure of massively intertwined networks of trust that shape values and politics.

A counter-intuitive social fact is that the actual structure of any organization or tribe is not a hierarchy, but a network. Networks exhibit reciprocity, an alchemy of mutual give and take between people eventually turning into a golden trust – and trust is the catalyst of change. For example, how do executives ensure long lasting change in their organizations? They must first map the network to locate the key holders of trust, because in the ensuing drama or trauma often associated with change, the trust in a network will always trump the authority of a hierarchy.

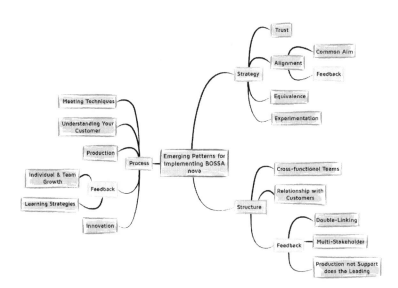

Emerging Patterns for Implementing BOSSA nova

The mind map above shows the individual patterns as they emerged from Part II into the strategy-structure-process meta pattern. This chart is a way of clustering concepts and concerns, and it does not mean, for example, that trust is a strategy.

The values don't show up in this diagram. Just as we mixed the four BOSSA nova streams of development in the end-of-chapter syntheses for each value, the patterns now mix the values. Like mixing hydrogen and oxygen, you get something with totally different characteristics: water. Similarly, these patterns are now something with a totally different characteristic. The streams of development are still there, the values are still there, but they are now in a compound form and ready to apply. From the strategy, structure, process meta pattern we get the background you need as a basis for formulating experiments, as we describe in the next section.

Start Experimenting

We realized that to make the meta pattern useful, we would need an approach designed to make it applicable. As discussed in Chapter 1, companies live today in a volatile, uncertain, complex, and ambiguous (VUCA) world. According to Cynefin, managing in complex environments calls for an approach of "probe, sense, respond" (see Kurtz & Snowden). In other words, if you face a complex situation, there is no recipe or formula you can follow. You can make reliable predictions in complicated situations but not in complex ones. Rather than simple recipes, we will suggest probes to help you start experimenting to test possible solutions. The probes can be used either as-is (if appropriate) or as an inspiration for your own best-fit probe. Note, there is no failure, because no matter if the probe is failing or succeeding, the emphasis is always on the learning. Thus, you need to stress that the goal is learning not that the probe will be a success. This marks the probe as being safe-to-fail.

For each pattern, we suggest a typical probe and accompanying example experiments for sensing and responding. Each probe provides first some background information including sample scenarios. The background is followed by an hypothesis which is a basis for the experiment. For each experiment we suggest a procedure, a measurement and thoughts about how to proceed after the experiment.. The results should lead you into the next step in your implementation of BOSSA nova. Generally, keep on probing to see if the patterns and benefits indicated by the diverse experiments exist at a larger scale and can be replicated and generalized.

In a number of these experiments it will be necessary to measure intangibles, and we make suggestions about how to do so. For further guidance on measuring intangibles we recommend Hubbard's *How to Measure Anything* (Hubbard). If the experiment doesn't support the hypothesis or gives mixed results, you need to reflect. Then, develop a different hypothesis that probes different perspectives relevant for your specific situation and test possible patterns with new experiments.

And note, we encourage you to begin experimenting as soon as you read this book. As the pattern *Just Do It* described by Manns and Rising's suggests, don't wait for the perfect moment when you have the resources and knowledge you think you need; instead, take the first baby step and start learning. (see Manns & Rising)

Insights from Hendrik Esser, Ericsson

At Ericsson we started early agile adoption in 2006 and went full-bore in 2010. At that time I worked in the leadership team of a 2000 person international organization. We used a mixture of Scrum-of-Scrum and a homemade portfolio management process to manage our complete product development. Our core ideas and needs were to decentralize decision making and truly embrace change. While Scrum and Scrum-of-Scrum were known concepts and relatively easy to adopt, the Portfolio Management process was a challenge. It started with a workshop into which I called all stakeholders of Product Development: Product Management, Product Development, Test, System Design, Deployment. In that workshop we went straight to the main issue we had at that time: all our releases were significantly delayed. Through an intensive debate we found two core problems: Product Management could not predict what customers would need in the future, and Product Development could not predict precisely how much effort would be required to develop a feature before feature development started. Based on this insight, we created a process that uses ranges for estimates of cost and time. These ranges are an expression of our uncertainty at a certain point in time. We agreed that using ranges is a good way to communicate the current best knowledge.

When implementing this approach, we of course faced some adoption issues as several people who had not been part of the workshop did not understand the idea behind the ranges. But as a communication tool they are meant to stir up discussions ("What do you mean: the delivery is between August and November? The customer needs it in July!"). The new approach gently directed us into the mindset shift we wanted. That shift took us in total about a year and a half.

We conducted a retrospective on why our transformation was successful. (In retrospectives, it is good to not only focus on why something didn't work out, but also why something worked!). Our reflections led us to find Human System Dynamics, VUCA and Complexity Management including the Cynefin Framework and the related experimentation approach.

We also learned that focusing on communication and continuous retrospectives at the leadership/organizational level are key ingredients for driving change. We formulate change experiments (knowing that there will be always side-effects) and monitor whether they lead to the desired outcome via retrospectives. We have since then started many more such initiatives.

Today, we understand, that if we want to unleash the full potential of the people in our organization, they need autonomy to take own decisions and drive things forward. However, we also understand, that individual autonomy ends in chaos if there is not sufficient alignment. The next question is: who is driving that alignment? We try to avoid "ivory towers" to create policies that are meant to align the organization. We rather focus on having the right level of participation: people affected by a regulation (strategies, common processes, etc.) need to be part of creating them. A concrete example is the way we today work with our development processes, driven via a Community of Practice structure. These communities are cross-organizational and fully empowered to take decisions within their area.

Diagnose Your Organization

To find a starting position for your experimental journey, you can use the diagnostic tools we mentioned in Chapter 2 including the Viable Systems Model and Agile Fluency Model (see Beer and Agile Fluency), Human Systems Dynamics, and Cynefin. There are many other tools you can use in the sort of thought process Hendrik Esser describes. We particularly suggest that you consider Organization Structure Canvas[3], the Kepner-Tregoe method, appreciative inquiry, SWOT (strengths, weaknesses, opportunities, threats) (see Mulder, Cooperrider, and SWOT), and the sociocracy process of "picture forming" as suggested in the probe Can group reflection improve problem solving? in Chapter 10. All these tools provide support for defining an area for you to start experimenting.

---

[3] https://medium.com/the-ready/the-os-canvas-8253ac249f53

We alert you again: we are mentioning these diagnostic tools so that you are aware they exist! You can learn about them if you want. The list might remind you of some tools that are already in your toolbox ready to use. Yet, you can also just start with one experiment that "speaks to you" without using any diagnostic tools.

Keep Reflecting

Where do probes come from? They emerge from reflection. We, therefore, strongly suggest that you develop your skills of reflection. Please try the following reflections exercise right now!

Start your reflections process by answering the following questions. Take the time to write down your answers.

1. How did I react to the request to reflect?
2. (Without peeking!) What do I recall as being the most important challenges for companies from Chapter 1?
3. Now, glance over Chapter 1 and note what challenges you remembered and what you didn't. . Reflect on: why didn't I remember those other challenges? To what extent were the challenges I remember also the challenges that are most important to my context? If there is a difference, why did I remember challenges that aren't so important to my context?

Note that the first question is "How did I react to the request to reflect?" For example, it's likely that you had a mixture of thoughts and feelings ranging from "how interesting" to "oh, blah, that's too much work. I'll just glance over what they wrote and keep going - I haven't got time for it." Or you might have thought "I bought this book; so, they should tell me." You might also have admired the idea, thinking "how innovative" and at the same time you might have thought, "Yuck! Sounds like something that my teacher in third grade made me do!"

Please write these thoughts and feelings down right now!! They likely all happened in a mere second. BEFORE you read further, write them down even if on a napkin or the back of a grocery store receipt.

.... (these dots mean we're waiting for you to do that) ;-)

So, let's dig in. If you haven't already done so, now answer questions 2 and 3.

.... (we're waiting)

Now that you've answered questions 2 and 3, stop again to reflect. Why are we asking you to proceed this way? It's because you actually can't think really new thoughts without some stillness and reflection (Fu Y1, Huang ZJ.) (Resnik).

For future reflections try posing questions about your situation or circumstances in the company, writing out your answers to these questions, and sharing your thoughts with your peers.

To apply BOSSA nova, start with reflection. The reflection will likely lead to new hypotheses that you can use to penetrate your situation and discern patterns that will lead to beneficial new strategies, structures, and processes.

In this Part, we will suggest many examples of possible experimental probes into various complex situations. And as you read through the probes, think about how they relate to your situation. Then try one or more experiments suggested by the most relevant probes, share the results with your peers, reflect again, and go onto the next probes. By following this loop you will continue implementing the BOSSA nova in deeper ways.

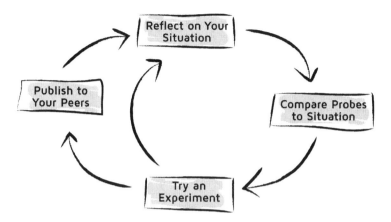

Keep Diving Deeper into BOSSA nova

8. Strategy

As we have seen above, from the institutional perspective *the company is an organization* or rather a social system with purpose that is guided by its strategy to provide value to customers. Chandler provides the most generally accepted definition of strategy: "Strategy is the determination of the basic long-term goals of an enterprise, and the adoption of courses of action and the allocation of resources necessary for carrying out these goals." (Chandler) The patterns that emerged for strategy from a company-wide Agility perspective are trust, alignment, equivalence, and experimentation.

8.1 Trust

Following are lessons we learned in Part II that are relevant to trust. They are drawn from the various values mentioned in parentheses:

- Trust in the wisdom of the individuals and their interactions, which means fewer rules and guidelines. They become semi-autonomous because they are not micromanaged. (Self-organization)
- Setting up rules and guidelines that assume all employees want to contribute positively to the company's success. (Self-organization)
- Self-organization creates trust. If the structures for encouraging self-organization are working well, then the level of trust should build over time. (Self-organization)

Probe: Do we need standardized metrics?

Background: A classic problem of large, successful organizations is that their bureaucracy becomes oppressive. The bureaucracy assumes that people are not inclined to use their common sense and are only looking for their own personal advantage. For example, if you are asked to report the status of your work as red, yellow, green, you will be tempted to favor yellow because green is risky - it could go wrong and then you'd be criticized. And, red draws too much attention.

Hypothesis: Standardized reporting procedures give the illusion of an accurate picture of what's actually happening. Self-reporting would let us see what is actually happening. A trusting approach would simply ask people to provide their own metric - something that reflects, from their perspective, what is actually happening and what needs to be shared.

Experiment: Set aside a time for members of a reporting unit, including the person they report to, to reflect on how they might be able to describe in succinct ways how to let the others know what is actually happening with their work and them to get feedback on what they are doing. They then report using metrics they develop individually. Try for two months and then have a retrospective with everyone involved, including the manager, that asks: "Do we want to continue this way of reporting?"

Probe: Is trust cheaper?

Background: Another example of oppressive bureaucracy is intricate travel expense controls that assume people will try to scam the company (only this kind of hotel, no more than this amount for food, etc).

Hypothesis: Travel cost controls are frustrating and deliver the mixed and off putting message: "although we trust you to make many important decisions, we also think you might cheat us." This mixed message demoralizes and the procedures actually cost more money and time than they save.

Experiment: For a specific period of time like three months, change travel budget constraints for a few units of the company. Set policies about how to deal with any obvious individual infractions, as may be needed. For example, a company we know of has only three guiding principles for travel expenses (and no other cost controls):

- The travel spending has to be economically sensible.
- Only ask for travel reimbursement that meets government legal and audit requirements.
- Take care of yourself.

In this example, it is up to the individual how much he or she will spend for the travel. For transparency, make records of travel expenditures available to everyone (which provides some peer control, e.g., if the expenses are sensible.) After taking a baseline measurement of the staff's level of frustration with travel cost controls, provide training about the rationale and values of the new trust-based way of controlling travel costs. If possible, match each experimental unit with a similar "control group" department that continues to use the old system. How much difference is there in actual expenditures and attitudes? Should the trust approach be continued and expanded?

8.2 Alignment

Do you find yourself in one of the following situations:

- Have you been losing customers you've had for a long period of time?
- Do you have troubles finding new customers?
- Do people of any one team pull together or are they squabbling and working against each other?

How can you probe the situation to see where your best leverage points are to deal with the situation? We will look into some typical hypotheses you might pose and test.

Common Aim

In Part II we explored:

- Self-organization is sparked by a common aim, challenge, equivalence, and/or shared values. These define the container; thus, the aim and values have an impact on the width or narrowness of the container. (Self-organization)
- The container is stronger if the aim is based on the customer's needs because the customer brings in an outside pressure or force that drives the self-organization phenomena. (Self-organization)
- Ensure that the customer focus is the aim, the reason for people working together as a team (in contrast to worry about the shareholders). (Constant customer focus)
- Ensure your budgeting approach is flexible toward customer and market needs. Do not fix the budget long-term upfront; make budgeting fit the customer focus. (Constant customer focus)

Probe: Can we improve collaboration by changing the incentive system?

Background: The overall strategic aim defines both an objective but also a boundary for objectives. For example, the manager who maneuvers for months to get a bigger corner office or another person who manipulates the "system" to get a promotion for a relative in another department are examples of a drift away from a common aim focused on the customer. In all these cases members of the organization are not collaborating but are focusing on a personal advantage. Other people might simply be working in a disengaged way, showing up at the office but wishing they were somewhere else and doing their work in a mechanical, "just enough to get by" manner.

Hypothesis: The reason people are not collaborating effectively is that their individual objectives are not aligned. Everyone is trying to reach his / her own objective and not the shared one of the team, department, or company. If reaching the individual objectives is rewarded with a bonus then the risk is even higher that every individual will look only for his / her personal advantage and not for the company's advantage. Therefore, if we (1) change our incentive systems (i.e. performance reviews, bonuses, appreciations, recognitions, and the like) and if we (2) separate monetary reward from performance review and promotions, people will support each other better and learn from one another. This mutual support or, in other words, this improved collaboration will better serve the customers' needs.

Experiment: A way to probe the hypothesis would be to have people in one typical group create and model what it would be like to have different incentive systems - Open Space methods might be helpful in designing their incentive system. Whatever conclusion they reach, have that group start using the new system for a period of 3 months. Possibilities we have heard of include: no one has a personal office, using "gaming points" to reflect personal learning and development achievements (see Shen and Hsee), having periodic "appreciations parties," pooling the bonus money and deciding as a whole what to do with it, peer reviews and stack ranking (see Valve), etc. Also, identify a roughly similar group as a control, thus creating the basis for an "A/B test."

A simple way to measure level of collaboration would be to ask each member of both the experimental and the control group to keep private reflections journals about how they are experiencing the group's collaboration (the "flow" in the group). At the end of e.g., three months ask each person to review their journal and, on a joint "collaboration seismograph", record their perception of level of collaboration. They can perhaps annotate or verbally comment on peaks and valleys of the graph. The collective graph will give a rough measure of changes in collaboration and indicate how well the incentive structure is supporting collaboration and thus alignment toward the common aim.

If the experiment's results indicate improved collaboration with the new incentive, expand to other groups. Consider running similar experiments by measuring not only internal collaboration but effectiveness in serving customers' needs.

Probe: Can peer decision-making about promotion support alignment?

Background: In our research we were unable to find any company in which there wasn't a hierarchy. Some aspects of work are hierarchical in nature - levels of abstraction, accumulation of skills in learning, seniority, natural leadership. Even at very egalitarian companies like Valve and Red Hat there are hierarchies and these require a promotion system. One type of promotion is domain related ("I am a senior coach in my domain.") and the other is people related, as in natural leadership. In one example we observed, a company that went through an agile transformation decided to give up on titles. The result was that people felt, "I'm going nowhere in my career. I feel stuck." Many started leaving to escape that stuck feeling. This outcome is not surprising as it is exactly what Herzberg predicts in his well-established two-factor motivation theory. (see Herzberg, Mausner & Snyderman).

Promotion is very complex because if you are operating as a team, which is an aspect of work that is egalitarian and social in nature,

- How do you pick out one person and give them a promotion?
- Who grants the promotion? Typically it is a top down decision. People apply for jobs and one person is selected by an executive or an executive committee discusses and makes appointments.

- What is the criteria for the promotion? Is it related to customer satisfaction or to pleasing the person who gives you the promotion? (e.g., should the customer give the promotion?)
- What does promotion mean? More money, higher prestige, career path, and/or a way to compare myself with others inside and outside the company?

Because there is such complexity, there is no one recipe. For example, Spotify reports interesting experiments with titling and career paths based on peer identification of expertise. Yet, they warn against copying what they are doing because they are constantly changing and customizing to their own culture.

Hypothesis: If we use peer decision making to make decisions about promotions, we can separate performance review from decisions such as promotion that have an element of competition. In other words, the competition becomes "cooperative competition." This approach will foster all of the values: foremost transparency, but also continuous customer focus, self-organization, and continuous learning. For example, everyone will know why and how the promotion decision was made and as a consequence will accept the outcome. It is important that before the decision process starts, everyone mutually develop the criteria that define the qualifications for promotion. Further, the process will have the creativity that comes with self-organization.

Experiments: Groups at different levels of the hierarchy in the company use:

- Sociocratic election to determine who is appointed for a promotion.
- Consent decision making on the person being promoted from a pool of applicants.
- Consent decision making for aligning individual and team objectives.

- Consent decision making for deciding on bonuses.

All of these experiments would proceed in a similar way. We'll discuss one of them in more detail as an example for all - the sociocratic election to determine who receives a promotion. Before starting the sociocratic election, identify an open position where the area of consideration for promotion to it is within the group and establish the responsibilities, authority, term, etc. The position could, for example, be for a senior technical position such as "Distinguished Engineer" or a management position. Invite the members of the group to a meeting arranged for the purpose of selecting someone to the position. If it is a management position, the group should include the person to whom the position will report as well as those who will report to the new person. As needed, train them on the sociocracy election process. Provide a facilitator, or if they are using sociocracy use their current facilitator.

 The following describes the sociocracy election process. It is useful in a variety of settings.

1. Review the responsibilities, authority, accountability, and associated salary, term in the position, and associated skills and knowledge.
2. Everyone individually writes on a piece of paper their name, the word "nominates," and the name of the person proposed for the position. They can propose themselves, someone else in the group, or abstain.
3. The facilitator collects all papers, selects one, and reads it outloud with a request for reasons. E.g., "George nominates Susan. George, please tell us why you are nominating Susan." The facilitator selects the next paper, repeats the same request for reasons, and continues until all the nominations have been presented.

4. Hold a "change round" in which the facilitator asks each person in turn, "Having heard the reasoning for the nominations, do you wish to change your nomination?" If a person wishes to change their nomination, the facilitator asks the person to give their reasons for changing.
5. The facilitator proposes one of the nominees, giving reasons for doing so. The facilitator might not propose the person who received the most nominations but rather weighs the arguments presented. The number of nominations is just one of the arguments to be considered.
6. The facilitator holds a consent round in which each person is asked in turn, "Do you have any paramount objection to the person proposed?" asking the proposed person last. If there are no objections, the facilitator announces that the group has consented to the proposed person taking the position and the group celebrates the decision.
7. If there is an objection, the facilitator goes back to each person who has objected and asks their reasons. The objection is not a veto but the beginning of a creative process that ensures all voices are heard and accounted for as the group together develops solutions that address the objection.

Measurement could be a pre-survey of the group to assess their opinion about the company's promotion policies including their transparency, quality of selections made, and objectivity. Give this survey also to some control group(s). Immediately after the election process is completed, collect spontaneous feedback, and then again for example three months later along with a post survey for the experimental and control group(s). If satisfaction improves, extend this process to other promotions.

Collective Ownership

The new synthesis from Part II supports collective ownership in the following way:

- Allow the people working together to follow their passion for doing work that matters and delights their customers. Thus, organize to honor passion bounded by responsibility. (Constant customer focus)
- Organize to serve your customer. Organize each facet of the company around coordinating services offered to any one customer. The kind of work and the customer's convenience should drive the review and reallocation of resources, not the calendar. (Constant customer focus)

Probe: How can we have autonomy as a team while supporting the organization's purpose?

Background: Your team is not focusing on the things that are the most important, but is coming up with one idea after another one.

Hypothesis: Although the team is self-organizing very well, there is no clear understanding about the purpose of the team or, in other words, there is passion which is not bound by responsibility for the common aim. In this case the overall goal (which is most likely serving the needs of a customer) is not clearly understood. Giving direct exposure to the customer will focus the team on customer needs.

Experiment: Establish a closer connection with the customer so the team can understand (and at best experience) the actual need of the customer. Arrange for some team members to walk and work with the customers and learn about their demands by experiencing the customers' work themselves. The expected result is that the team will come up with better ideas for solving the customer's needs and greater understanding of the team's common aim. If so, make the approach of walking and working with their customers a practice for all teams.

Insights from Todd Kromann, Walmart

A tiny cohort of four agile coaches was able to invite thousands of IT employees and contractors at Walmart to shift the organization's work from 10% agile to 90% agile in less than two years. We simply invited the people doing the work into Open Space, in more than 30 one-day events, hundreds at a time.

We didn't impose a methodology, a tool or a metric. We offered invitation, autonomy, and options. We asked everyone to find ways to make their work more agile. That was the purpose and all the ideas went up on the wall, completely open and transparent. As the work took off, "Agile Champions" helped the four coaches spread the invitation and the results.

Formally, the business adopted agile concepts such as founder's mentality, design thinking and Team of Teams. These were promoted from the CEO level and the IT coaches had little involvement. Walmart has several agile 'thought leaders' on it's board of directors and they contributed to the net effect.

Because this was very open, the story is hard to define. The scope could be as low as 4000 or into the 10's of thousands depending on who you ask. The Bentonville business departments were included (it was open) and business folks usually opted to attend.

Today, I get reference checks for Agile coaches from Walmart, and these are often people I've never met. Any of our champions claim that title. I think that's a side effect of an open transformation. So, the concept of 4 coaches is only correct in the narrow sense of 4 people whose full time job was coaching. By the end we scaled up to 6 full time coaches in Bentonville and perhaps a dozen worldwide. This was federated so, again, it's hard to define.

While the numbers are hard to pin down, the net effect is not. We are now 100% agile in that it's more awkward to opt out than to opt in. We no longer have any Agile coaches. If you ask anyone at Walmart how we became agile, they will likely say they did it by themselves ;) An open transformation is like an avalanche. It just takes a few snowballs and after that, it's chaos.

Probe: How can we leverage the existing network?

Background: According to Karen Stephenson in every company there are many trust networks in place for different kinds of work. The leaders of these networks often powerfully influence the dynamic structure of the company see Chapter 7. Can we directly address this often hidden leadership structure to get assistance in building alignment?

Hypothesis: If we identify hidden trust leaders and get them together, they will, together, be able to improve the company's alignment for customer focus.

Experiment: Conduct surveys to determine "who in the company do we trust the most regarding our relationships with our customers?" The survey process should identify persons who "know how the system really works," "won't blab if I share a problem or mistake with them," "have a good relationship with the customers," and/or "intuits the customers' needs." The persons identified are now visible. They build the trust network that aligns for customer focus. Introduce the people identified to each other and invite them participate in an ad hoc cross-functional team. The team builds the company's culture by coming up with improvements such as decreasing the response time for customers' requests, repeating business, or minimizing waste (e.g. unsold inventory, unnecessary or too complicated processes, output rather than outcome, etc.) All of these improvements should pre- and post-measured.

Feedback

In Part II we recommended:

- Have performance reviews, individual goals, and incentives aligned with the customer focus. The strategy is to focus feedback systems on customer needs and not on other needs such as shareholders. (Constant customer focus)
- Separate individual objectives from bonus. (Continuous learning)

Probe: Is there an alternative to short-term profit focus?

Background: The board notes that long term customers are leaving although you are still attracting new customers. What is the cause of this "customer churn"?

Hypothesis: We are damaging our long term profitability by focusing on quarterly profits and cutting costs and services to keep boosting immediate profit. If we release a selected department from our latest cost cutting, they will get long term customers to return and customer attrition will diminish.

Experiment: The conventional way of finding out more about the cause of customer churn would be to survey long-term customers who have left and those who haven't. But, such methods can be expensive and may not be reliable - and certainly not creative. Another approach to gain insight could be to hold a simulation in which customers participate or the team creates a persona that approximates customer reactions to various scenarios. Besides being less expensive, this approach could open more possibilities for new ideas. One design for the experiment might be to have a set of role players who are from a "scenario department" that is cutting costs and another set of people who are in a "scenario department" that is not implementing anticipated cost cutting.

Have a third set of people play the "customer personas" for both department scenarios so that there is some consistency in the customer personas. The measurement would focus on the personas team's subjective reports on their different experiences with the two scenario departments. Reports of the scenario department players plus those of independent observers would give perspective to the reactions of the persona players.

There are several possible variations. For example, the customer personas could be new customers and established customers. Do the new customers get a better deal than the current customers? The authors have personal experience with their phone companies where new customers get special deals but the company never offers the same deal to current customers.

The decision might be to do the cost cutting, but the role play experience might modify the cost cutting strategy to avoid any negative effects identified during the experiment. Or, maybe the decision will be to put off the cost cutting in the expectation that the amounts saved would be more than offset by new revenue.

Probe: Will aligned individual growth happen without motivation by a bonus?

Background: Often individual objectives are not revisited and if the market changes, the objectives might become out of date. If the objective doesn't reflect that market change and further if it is tied to a bonus, the person will still work toward that objective even if it has become meaningless. We have observed situations such as: a software developer who pushes the team toward using a specific programming language, even though it doesn't fit the purpose of the actual project. His performance plan says he will get a bonus if he learns that programming language!

Hypothesis: If we separate bonus/incentive payments from the learning process, individual growth will happen in alignment with the company's strategy.

Experiment: Begin the experiment by identifying two similar units that are using a bonus system connected to individual objectives and determining which will be the experimental unit and which the control. Get consent from both units to participate in the experiment. Do pre-measures consisting of self-reflective notes as well as objective indicators of performance, both individual and unit level. Then, in the experimental unit introduce different formats to recognize accomplishment of new skills. Discontinue using a bonus system connected to individual objectives for the experimental unit (instead, e.g., distribute the available bonus equally among the members of the unit). If you have changing conditions, increase the frequency of performance evaluations weekly, monthly, quarterly (see Ismael et al). Moreover, use qualitative Objectives and quantitative Key Results (OKR). The OKR are defined bottom up rather than in traditional way, i.e., Balanced Scorecards where individual objectives are defined top-down. Yet, similar to Balanced Scorecards, OKRs are always a contribution to the company's overall goal, which will ensure the alignment to the company's strategy.

As an example of OKRs, an individual objective one salesperson might choose could be getting better at empathetic connections. Another salesperson might want to know more about the product line. A third person's objective could be getting better in bridging between customer needs and the people who create the product by learning to speak both their languages. Sample key results for the latter objective could be:

- Spend a day every other month accompanying your customer his or her daily business to observe their needs.
- Spend a day every other month accompanying someone from your company's product design or manufacturing team to observe their challenges.
- Give a conceptual presentation to the company's product designers, first in the customer's language and then translated

into the language of the company's product designers.

- Attend similar presentations by your peers.

In performance reviews for both the control and experimental units, guide the discussion with the following kinds of questions, remembering that serving the customer better is a side benefit:

- What did you learn?
- How did you learn it?
- What do you intend to learn next?
- What did you learn from your peers?
- How do the OKRs and the performance review help or hinder your learning?

Do a post measurement of both the experimental and control unit using the same parameters as the pre-measure, again on the individual and unit level. Compare the results. Do the experimental unit results indicate lower, the same, or higher individual growth? What do you and the participating units think the company should do with the results? For example, if it's working well, expand to more units. If the results are ambiguous, what did we learn and do we want to try another experiment with different parameters?

Insights from Eric Abelen, ING, Netherlands

Performance management as key driver of ING Bank's agile enterprise transformation

Summer 2015, headquarters of ING[a] in The Netherlands embarked on a massive organization wide adventure: Kicked off by a spectacular big bang event in Amsterdam's Ajax soccer stadium, the organisation morphed into Spotify-inspired agile Tribes and Squads, and adopted a related agile way of working. Find a short video explaining key concepts of ING's way of working on Youtube[b]. As it is one of the few examples of an agile transformation attempted at such big scale, lots has been published about it. See for example McKinsey[c], and Mary Poppendieck[d]. The Dutch ING organisation is now some two years on its agile route, and it is achieving good results. So far, so good.

The unfolding changes at the Dutch ING organization have now inspired reinvention of the way-of-working at all ING entities worldwide. Summer 2017, ING's CEO Ralph Hamers announced ING's ambition to become *a digital bank; an IT company delivering banking services*. This IT company will fundamentally adopt an agile way of working, driven from the belief that this approach will reduce time to market and respond faster to changing customer needs; that it will reduce obstacles and handovers to give room and empower individuals and teams; and that it will develop more motivated, passionate and self-starting employees.

Now ING's Netherlands-tested agile way-of-working will be challenged to expand, renew and reinvent itself to function in other ING country organizations, each with their unique geographical culture. The company will have to 'learn and adapt' at a scale not seen before. It promises to be a very exciting journey that will positively and fundamentally impact ING's already very change and action oriented corporate culture.

ING's corporate culture today can perhaps best be described by the "Orange Code"; a 'home-grown' set of enterprise-wide values and behaviours that function as the code of conduct in the company worldwide. ING's key values are: being honest, prudent, and responsible. Behaviours associated with these values are: "you take it on and make it happen", "you help others to be successful", and "you are always a step ahead". This Orange Code can easily be linked to the Agile Principles, which are of great help in integrating an agile mindset into the existing corporate culture. In ING's selection and appraisal processes, employees are ranked against this Orange Code to facilitate an improvement dialogue. That is, linking Orange Code to Agile Principles is an effective lever to drive needed discussion and reflection.

This linkage is important because appraisal systems are key levers for sustainable success. In ANY agile transformation, performance management is a challenging topic. But when scaling up towards worldwide intra-company agile collaboration, it might even become the key success factor for sustainable success.

Performance Management is tricky for the simple reason that it is a feedback system in itself and, therefore, gets close to 'the ego'. Mindset drives behaviour, and behaviour is strongly influenced by the feedback system and remuneration culture one functions in. To grow a global agile enterprise culture, ING's transformation also will have to reinvent the way we value and rate contributions of everybody involved.

To-date, contributions of ING employees are rated via a Job Career Framework, job scales, and a process of yearly performance target setting, coaching, and rewarding (including the aforementioned Orange Code elements). In essence, this yearly target setting is an 'old fashioned, non-agile' approach because it does not stimulate an ongoing performance dialogue and 'growth mindset' (learning by doing, overcoming failure, based on the intrinsic desire to get better). The current performance management process offers the option to include learnings and change objectives mid-year, but that option requires a pretty well developed agile mindsets of both employee and manager. To drive the envisioned cultural change, ING's enterprise appraisal system will get adjusted in the coming years to better encourage a 'growth mindset' and related value of reiterative 'learning by doing'.

In already agile inspired departments of ING Netherlands, teams are encouraged to include team-agreements in the appraisal rounds: A team collectively defines its appraisal objective, tracks progress (key to driving ongoing performance dialogue), and by the end of the appraisal period the full team is ranked against that self-defined criteria via a group (retrospective) session. All team members get the same score on that item or items. Combined with scoring on the other defined individual criteria, the final appraisal score is set. At IT-centred sections of ING Netherlands, deciding on promotions has become a full departmental activity. During so called yearly 'Performance Days' all employees reporting within the IT section participate in a performance review cycle that includes a department-wide calibration of candidates for promotion, based on the Dreyfus model of expertise levels.

These are certainly good developments, but for the moment they are rather isolated from each other. Corporate HR is working on standardising performance management policies globally, but this will take time as HR will need time to grasp fully what it takes to support an agile organisation and also because focus on global harmonisation is a relatively new phenomenon to this company. ING has never been run like a multinational. Local ING entities have been managed as rather independent entities. It is only since CEO Hamers' Think Forward strategy (that now includes the envisioned agile inspired culture) that we have put full focus on the corporate collective and the benefits of collaboration between ING entities across national borders.

And as long as an agile mindset is not yet systemically ingrained in ING's corporate culture, the reporting structure of ING local (country) entities could hinder that needed cross-border collaboration because local reporting structures can stimulate silo-forming and thus hinder growth of an agile sharing & learning mindset across entities. From a mindset perspective, the key principles of 'agile' definitely are not alien to a commercial environment, yet ARE often regarded as such. This means that in some sections of the company a very real paradigm shift in thinking and related culture, as well as processes, will be needed especially where it includes enterprise appraisal systems between respective ING country organisations. This cross-country aspect is another reason why we need to address this change very systemically at all levels of the organisation.

All in all, defining a 'performance management' system that systemically encourages, instead of hurting agile culture, is a big and crucial hurdle to overcome on our journey towards ING's enterprise agility worldwide. Looking at the company's DNA and it's great history of being able to drive successful change fast, I am confident that we will jump that fence. Once we atune autonomy with alignment, systemically and authentically in ALL segments and ALL layers of this digital-izing enterprise, we will have become that flexible, customer focused agile IT company delivering banking services.

[a]https://www.ing.com/web/show

[b]https://www.youtube.com/watch?v=NcB0ZKWAPA0

[c]http://www.mckinsey.com/industries/financial-services/our-insights/ings-agile-transformation

[d]http://www.leanessays.com/

8.3 Equivalence

In Part II we discovered:

- Make information available and accessible to the people who need it to do their work. (Transparency)
- All necessary information is shared. (Transparency)
- Self-organizing teams have all the information needed to deliberate a topic. (Transparency)
- Creating equivalence - an equal voice for everyone involved. (Self-organization)

Probe: What would happen if we emphasized transparency company-wide?

Background: Imagine that you have a large team that you need to split into four or five sub teams focusing on different business domains. You discuss it openly with everyone involved and jointly develop a way of accomplishing the split using self-selecting teams. But, there is a secret. There is another team in the company that will be dissolved - but with no layoff. This information is confidential because no one knows exactly what will happen when the dissolution occurs and HR is afraid people will leave before they can develop attractive offers. Some of the people are likely to want to join one of the five new subteams. If they do, the self-selecting process will change because the team dynamics will be different. Once the information is out, the self-selection will change. If all this information is sprung on both teams, the impact is likely to be rumors flying beforehand and a negative impact on trust and commitment to the organization. This situation could be an opportunity to see the effects of transparency in a "safe-to-fail" way.

Hypothesis: If we tell the team being dissolved what is going on and invite them to develop ideas for how to handle the dissolution process, and if we tell the team being split what is happening, few if any people will leave and the level of trust and commitment will rise in the units directly affected as well as other related parts of the organization.

Experiment: Do a pre-measure of morale, satisfaction, and commitment in the overall division that both units belong to. Call a meeting of the unit being dissolved, make the commitment of the company explicit by informing everyone that the company wants to keep everyone and intends to find new positions that they will find attractive. Collect everyone's input on how to accomplish that objective. Formulate a plan from these ideas that everyone consents to. For example, a plan might emerge to form a subcommittee to work with HR. Then, hold a meeting with the unit being split and request that they modify their self-selection process already developed (but not yet executed). After the process is complete, repeat the measurement of morale, satisfaction, and commitment. Include the question, how could we have handled this process differently? Note how many people actually leave the company from the unit being dissolved and hold in-depth exit interviews with any who do leave to understand why. Hold a retrospective to go over the results. Should such experiments be expanded to other parts of the company?

8.4 Experimentation

We learned in Part II:

- Define an hypothesis first, then experiment around this hypothesis and learn from the results - which then feed into the next hypothesis. (Continuous learning)
- Focus on the aim (customer focus) of the company and promote not just training but also teaching and organized research. Organized research includes sharing or publishing what you are learning with peers so that they can attempt to replicate and validate your conclusions. (Continuous learning)
- Use failure as a learning opportunity and make the learning transparent and independent of the function in the organizational structure. (Continuous learning)
- Make your work and the progress toward the result transparent. (Transparency) It is often uncomfortable information, yet if you don't know about it, you can't act on it. (Transparency)
- Information is based on verifiable facts (like a concrete delivery). (Transparency)
- Use an MVP, a minimum viable product, for testing the waters. (Constant customer focus)

Probe: Can we be more scientific?

Background: As we noted in Part II, the scientific process expects that you will do a literature search as part of your process of developing an hypothesis. It also requires you to write and submit your results for peer review and publication. We are unaware of any company that supports a full scientific process around its management and governance systems. If it hires scientists in its technical areas of work, they are likely to be encouraged to publish and attend scientific conferences, but only technical scientists get such encouragement. As a result, companies all over the world are trying to learn the same lesson in isolation from each other - and in fact units of the same company are unlikely to be sharing the learnings from their experimentation. This situation is, needless to say, wasteful.

In the BOSSA nova disciplines, we find that only the Agile Alliance supports a full exchange of learnings experiments following the scientific approach (see AgileAlliance Experience Reports). Open Space, Beyond Budgeting, and Sociocracy in one way or another encourage publication, but the publications are not peer reviewed or easily accessible. Within companies our experience is that something approaching the scientific publication process occurs only where there is extensive use of Agile - but only in some companies.

Hypothesis: If we set up a peer-reviewed in-house journal for experimentation in management practices and encourage everyone in the company to search this journal before they try probing with experiments, we will find an increase in cross-company collaborative thinking. Furthermore, if we encourage publication of these papers (vetted to remove company sensitive information), we will also see more complete scientific processes in house.

Experiment: Set up a peer-reviewed in-house journal for reporting experiments in management practices with a "review by" date of nine months. If the number of articles contributed, the number of people interested in peer reviewing, and the number of hits on the journal increase during the nine months, then continue the journal.

Probe: Can we really learn from failure?

Background: Some top managers may say we want continuous learning but are reluctant to publish their own failures or say that they are uncertain about a given situation and are trying to learn from it. They need a way out of this "do as we say not as we do" trap so that they can be effective role models for the rest of the organization.

Hypothesis: If top management, including the board, issues a statement on some specific issue that talks about past mistakes and learnings from them and/or uncertainty about a situation and the hypotheses they came up with for dealing with it, the organization will develop a culture of accepting and learning from failure.

Experiment: Do a pre-measure of the extent to which the organization is transparent about uncomfortable information. The measure could include a spot check of published retrospectives (abstract summaries or even ones that are only "published" on flip charts in the work area). Another could be an assessment of repeated mistakes such as work not completed, ships misaddressed, same complaints from customers. And for the Board and top management, small indicators such as repeated agenda items, or topics revisited, or repeated instances of space not reserved on agendas for generative thinking, or larger indicators such as missed opportunities as indicated by "surprise" competitor initiatives or new markets. Then, issue three statements, two months apart, indicating mistakes made, lessons learned, uncertainty being experienced, and how they are probing that uncertainty. Repeat the pre-measures to see if there is a change. If the change is positive, keep reinforcing the new culture, eg., by finding ways of recognizing those who exemplify this new mode of behavior.

Experiment: The previous experiment could be tried on a smaller scale. For example, several managers could run a retrospective about their recent activities and publish their learnings by simply posting a couple of flip charts in a prominent area. The may even publish their conclusions from these meetings in the company wiki and hold periodic discussions of the conclusions across roles and hierarchies - maybe in an Open Space format. Measurements of effectiveness could be similar.

8.5 Reflection

Follow the format of Adaptive Action from Human Systems Design in Chapter 6, Continuous Learning (see also Eoyang & Holladay):

Please take some time to recap *what* different probes were in this Chapter.

.... (these dots mean we're waiting for you to do that) ;-)

So, what are your insights about those probes? Again note them down.

.... (we're waiting)

Now what do you consider as your next steps given your context? Which one speaks most to your current situation? What are your plans for trying something like it?

.... (we're waiting)

See you in a little while in the next Chapter!

.

9. Structure

From the instrumental perspective, *a company has an organization,* which is reflected in its structure. We will now explore the effects on the structure of implementing company-wide Agility.

9.1 Cross-Functional Teams

The summary from Part II:

- Cross-functionality for including all necessary and different perspectives. The variety in perspectives must be balanced with the common aim. (Self-organization)
- Use a cross-functional team so that the customer focus is understood from all angles (different perspectives). (Constant customer focus)
- Relying on self-selecting teams / groups emphasizes trust in the wisdom of the individuals and their interactions. (Self-organization)

Probe: Is cross-functionality actually useful?

Background: Cross-functionality often appears in traditional organizations only in crises when they create a task force consisting of everyone who knows about the crisis and give them carte blanche to solve the problem.

Hypothesis: We know how a cross-functional task force helps solve crisis problems, why not implement it as a regular practice?

Experiment: Identify a persistent, high importance but non-crisis problem and facilitate formation of a cross-functional team with relevant areas of expertise, and strongly empower the team to resolve it. In other words, they are fully supported by managers, managers get formalities out of the way, etc. Solving that problem should be the team's shared and only aim. Identify another problem as a "comparison problem" and don't change current responsibility for solving it. How quickly and with what quality does the problem get resolved as compared to the problem that didn't get a cross-functional team? Was the time invested by the cross-functional team worth the value of the problem? If the problem gets resolved more quickly than the "comparison problem," what was the value of the timeliness? If successful, how else can you try out the cross-functional team concept?

9.2 Relationship with Customer

In Part II we said:

- Establish a bidirectional relationship with your customer. (Constant customer focus)
- Consider establishing a product owner function to maintain the bidirectional relationship. (Constant customer focus)

Probe: Can reflective meetings improve customer relations?

Background: Regardless of type of business there needs to be reflective time spent considering how well are we serving the customer. The authors' experience is that if there is no "customer focus" time, we make assumptions about the customer that may or may not be true. Ultimately, it is impossible to maintain a high quality rapport with the customer.

Hypothesis: If we establish regular reflective meetings at every level of the organization (somewhat like we asked you to take time to reflect at the beginning of this Part), the quality of customer service will increase.

Experiment: In a few specific units of the organization, establish a rhythm of regular meetings to reflect on how well the unit is serving its customer. Have a product owner present, or designate someone to serve in that role. In determining what adaptations are needed for better service, make decisions only by consent. If possible, identify other related units as controls to have meetings but not reflective meetings with product owners present or who have no product owner. Compare the results of the experimental units and the control units by whatever customer satisfaction tool you commonly use such as net promoter score, focus groups, etc. If results prove positive, consider expanding the use of a product owner function and reflective meetings.

A variation of this experiment is the use of personas representing your customers.

9.3 Feedback

No structure, no feedback. The structure helps or hinders giving and getting feedback. Thus, feedback requires its own configuration that enables continuous learning across different teams, roles, and hierarchies.

Double-Linking

In Part II we said:

- Double-linking for creating a bottom-up link (next to the usual top-down link), which builds a feedback loop in a hierarchy. (Self-organization)
- Enable the board of directors to be open to feedback from and measurement by the customer. (Constant customer focus)

- The structure is to have representatives from the staff serve as full members on the board (double-link representative) - as well as outside representatives who have different perspectives on the customer. (Constant customer focus)
- Include the shareholders (Board) in the customer focus so that they don't stand outside the process. (Constant customer focus)

Probe: Can our board of directors have the CEO and an elected representative on it without interfering with the work of the board?

Background: There are many philosophies and even legal restrictions about who can be on a board of directors. For example, a traditional corporation board's membership is only representatives of shareholders. Some nonprofit theorists (see Carver) assert firmly that the CEO should be the servant of the board and not a member of the board. However, to be agile a board must receive feedback that it cannot ignore from the organization as well as stakeholders in addition to the shareholders. Even if the board is interested in improving its ability to collaborate by including different kinds of members, it may feel prohibited from doing so by its bylaws. However, the board can create room to experiment by using a parliamentary device known as a "committee of the whole." Any board can establish committees. Those committee can include people who are not members of the board. A committee of the whole includes all the board members. By meeting as a committee, they can have non-board members fully participating.

Hypothesis: A board can experiment with changes in its structure and membership even if those changes appear to be prohibited by regulation or its bylaws by using a "committee of the whole." With this adaptation, it can easily experiment with the use of double-linking.

Experiment: Establish a committee of the whole. Invite the CEO and an elected representative (the two double-links) and a few outside experts from key sectors of the organization's environment. Make decisions using consent. At the end of each meeting, have a one minute long official board meeting in which the members vote to adopt the decisions made by the committee of the whole. Use this format for at least three board meetings, carefully evaluating each meeting. If the evaluations are positive, look into ways to change the bylaws to adopt the new configuration and decision-making methods used in the committee of the whole on a permanent basis.

Insights from Pieter van der Meché, The Sociocracy Group

The consent principle alone is not enough to boost cooperation between organizational levels. There must be a double linked connection: both an operational leader and an elected representative. It is particularly valuable for unveiling and guiding tension between organizational layers around controversial topics. In one case, an organization's management had to sign a social plan with unions within two weeks. The plan had far reaching consequences for pensions, who is laid off first, etc. The CEO had only discussed it with her management team, and it was never shared in the general circle. The CEO hesitated to put it on the agenda because of the near deadline. "Suppose one of the representatives has a paramount objection? There is no time to deal with that." I advised her though to bring it up in the meeting and explain the time crunch. Keeping such a critical issue outside of the circle meeting would be a source of mistrust and doubt about whether management took the sociocratic structure seriously. So she did.

The first round made clear that representatives did not understand the plan, and that they did not know the organization was in such a bad financial shape. They were shocked. They feared also the reactions of their colleagues especially towards themselves as they would be co-responsible for possible unavoidable negative consequences of the social plan on their colleagues. Maybe this was something where they should not be involved. I stepped in. "You can very well leave the meeting or abstain from participating in the decision making on this topic. That would imply that you delegate the decision making to those that stay in. Which is okay but it is also something you will have to explain to your colleagues. Explain to them that you had the opportunity to steer the decision making in such a way that the final decision also had your consent but that you decided not too and let the others, read management, take the decision for you. Which means also giving up the power of your circle to influence the decision making in the general circle." The representatives decided to stay. They were even willing, if necessary to save the organization, to consent to the plan. Though they expected their colleagues to be upset, too, and that it could take months to calm them down. Seeing the distress of the representatives the CEO proposed to ask the unions to move the deadline to buy time. But how to bring the message to the rest of the organization in a way that it would be a stimulus to join forces to save jobs? Representatives proposed a meeting for all the employees where the CEO explained the difficult position the organization was in and explained the social plan. After the meeting, each circle would have time to discuss it themselves and feed the representative and leadership with information that they could bring back to the general circle meeting to make a sound decision. This was consented, executed and worked out fine.

What is the learning here? First of all that as CEO or as management team you miss critical information to realize the goal. In this case they did not know or underestimated the reaction of the people they led. Second that it was the combination of representatives, a circle meeting and the consent principle that enabled this information to be fed into the decision making process and improve the result. And third, for a decision to be effective you need to take into account the time it takes to produce a well-designed and accepted decision instead of focusing solely on a self-imposed deadline.

There is another learning in this case that has general meaning. The CEO hesitated to bring a crucial item to the circle: share the thinking to decide the issue. And the representatives did hesitate to take responsibility for solving the issue, to accept sharing the power to decide. Both had to make a step towards shared decision making and shared responsibility for the decisions. When they did, all gained because of the ability to produce better decisions and better cooperation. It is one of key transformations sociocracy can bring about. Experience tells us that this transformation is not done at once, i.e. by signing a 'constitution' or following a training. It is a process that takes time and needs support of experienced certified sociocratic experts who have been through this process themselves.

Multi-Stakeholder

Part II states:

- Establish multi-stakeholder control of the company. Address this fundamental issue by providing a specific legal structure to establish the multi-stakeholder environment. (Constant customer focus)

Probe: Should we change our legal structure?

Background: If you experimented with having the CEO, an elected representative, and outside stakeholders on the board, as we suggest earlier in this Chapter, you may want to take the next step and anchor this arrangement in your legal structure. Experimenting with changing your legal structure would be difficult because it is a big step, expensive to do, may have unknown consequences, and hard to undo once done.

Hypothesis: If we change our legal structure to incorporate BOSSA nova principles, there will be a big benefit from focusing the passion of the staff and their increased commitment to the company.

Experiment: We can probe this possible step by using our informal networks as a way to conduct *indirect* experiments that would be challenging for us to do by ourselves. Talking with our networks would be the equivalent of doing our own research. Research business community networks. Here are some examples of experiments with legal structures you might find valuable to consider in your own company:

- Benefit corporations: to minimize damage that can be done by hostile takeovers of local companies a number of states in the USA have created a form of corporation known as benefit corporations. This legal form allows corporations that provide measurable benefits to society to place people who are not representatives of shareholders on their board and to make decisions that are for the benefit of society and not necessarily in the best interests of the shareholders.
- Volkswagen Act: The state of Lower Saxony holds a voting share of 20.2 percent, which gives it the ability to veto major decisions and prevent takeovers by other shareholders, regardless of the extent of the ownership. It also allows the government of Lower Saxony to appoint two members to Volkswagen's board. (see VolkswagenAct)
- Sociocracy recommends a double corporation in which a conventional for-profit corporation issues one (or a minimum number of) controlling share of stock. A foundation controls that share. Other kinds of shares can receive dividends but do not have control. The members of the board of the foundation and the board of the corporation are identical and certify they will vote each matter identically. Both boards decide by consent. Thus, the corporation in essence owns itself and is immune from hostile takeovers.

- Limited liability companies are partnerships that provide the liability protection of a corporation. In the USA, the structure of LLCs is minimally regulated by the state. Thus, an LLC can write its operating agreement (equivalent of corporate bylaws) anyway the members wish.
- In the Netherlands there is an exemption from the law that requires works councils if the company is structured sociocratically. The rationale is that double linking ensures all employees from bottom to top are involved in policy decision making.

If you find attractive alternatives in your research, there may be ways to probe specific features of the new legal structures. For example, the probe discussed above, Can our board of directors have the CEO and an elected representative on it without interfering with the work of the board?

Insights from Jez Humble, DevOps Research and Assessment LLC

A common obstacle to adopting agile methods in large companies is procurement. The US federal government spends over $86bn annually on contracted IT projects. Most projects cost hundreds of millions of dollars, and take 5-10 years to build. When complete, these contracts often deliver systems that are late, not fit for purpose, or use technology that is obsolete by the time of delivery.

Rather than delivering projects in one big batch, some teams in the federal government have been using a practice known as modular procurement. In this paradigm, each contract is small, lasts a few months (six months is common), and delivers a working increment that delivers value.

18F, a consulting team within the General Services Administration, created a contract vehicle known as the Agile Blanket Purchase Agreement (BPA). To be able to do work under this agreement, vendors had to build a working prototype in the space of days, with their code open sourced and available on GitHub.

With contracts awarded under the Agile BPA, and in line with the principles of Beyond Budgeting, agencies work with vendors to get from solicitation to contract kickoff in weeks rather than months, and deliver a working system in a few months rather than years or never. The system can be extended and improved through additional task orders. All software created through the Agile BPA must be open source, and all development must occur in a public version control repository (the repository for the first product developed through the Agile BPA is available at https://github.com/truetandem/fedramp-dashboard).

New solicitations are posted at https://ads.18f.gov/, where the Agile BPA is summarized: "The most important thing for us is the ability to ship high-quality working software. We plan to issue task orders ... that feature shorter time-frames, smaller dollar amounts, and user-centered design principles." You can find more on modular procurement at https://modularcontracting.18f.gov/.

Production not Support does the Leading

In Part II we learned:

- Departments that provide support to the departments that directly serve the customer should collaborate and not control each other. (Constant customer focus)

Probe: Would it be worthwhile to establish mindful partnerships between production and support service teams?

Background: Many support service teams such as quality control, human resources, finance, and security tend to be more controlling than supporting and tend to come in too late in production processes. The (probably unfair) impression of the teams who directly serve the customer is that support services only operate from checklists like martinets and not by what needs to be done right now or what is needed with the particular customer.

Hypothesis: If support service teams understand that production is their direct customer, or in other situations if production understands that support service teams are their direct customer, they can be more proactive in working together production to serve the company's external customers.

Experiment: For a specific project, production invites the applicable support service teams at the very beginning of the project and treats them as stakeholders (see Larsen & Nies). It asks them to describe their needs. It prioritizes those needs just like any customer. Measure the results by asking "How is the support service team/production relationship going?" in every project retrospective. Record the comments in detail so that you have a journal for the experiment. You could also ground these comments with quantitative measurements such as lead or wait times.

In just such an experiment with a client, the authors heard the support service team say, "For the first time, our work seems appreciated." And, on the other hand, the production teams didn't experience the support service team any longer as a pain in the neck but rather as partners who help serve the company's external customers.

9.4 Reflection

Follow the format of Adaptive Action from Human Systems Design in Chapter 6, Continuous Learning (see also Eoyang & Holladay):

Please take some time to recap *what* different probes were in this Chapter.

.... (these dots mean we're waiting for you to do that) ;-)

So, what are your insights about those probes? Again note them down.

.... (we're waiting)

Now what do you consider as your next steps given your context? Which one speaks most to your current situation? What are your plans for trying something like it?

.... (we're waiting)

See you in a little while in the next Chapter!

10. Process

The functional perspective refers to how *the company is being organized*. We are looking at the processes and procedures that direct the daily work.

10.1 Meeting Techniques

In Part II we encouraged:

- Retrospectives for adapting the process (and structure) for the actual needs. (Self-organization)
- Decision-making procedures based on consent for creating equivalence - an equal voice for everyone involved. (Self-organization)
- Organize open meetings, where anyone who cares about the issue is invited to attend or even call the meeting, and the topic is the priority. Totally new things can emerge, and the schedule bends to that priority. (Self-organization)
- Picture forming is used to gather relevant information before developing solutions. (Transparency)
- A process is to include customer feedback in each board meeting. (Constant customer focus)

Probe: Can group reflection improve problem solving?

Background: Too often teams jump to solutions before they really understand the situation or the context, i.e, before they have a clear picture of the challenge they face or the opportunity before them.

They end up in a muddle, for example, coming up with solutions addressing the symptoms only, or addressing problems they don't really have. The real problems keep coming back. The authors, for example, have seen situations in software development where the retrospectives at the end of each sprint keep going over basically the same problems.

The discipline of picture forming before searching for solutions addresses the need to have a common understanding. "Picture forming" basically means group reflection. We started this Part encouraging personal reflection, but we could as well have encouraged group reflection. There are a number of tools for group picture forming including the Kepner-Tregoe method, appreciative inquiry, SWOT (strengths, weaknesses, opportunities, threats) (see Mulder, Cooperrider, and SWOT), and the Viable System Model for understanding and simplifying organizational systems (see Beer). Sociocracy suggests as another procedure: have each person in turn ("in a round") describe their view of the situation, record their comments on flip charts, organize the comments, and confirm that the group has a "good enough for now" picture.

Hypothesis: If we strictly enforce picture forming as the first step in addressing any opportunity or challenge, teams will accurately "nail the problem."

Experiment: Identify two teams representing a cross section of your company or unit. Pre-measure their understanding of problem solving by asking individuals in the teams to describe their team's problem solving process. Ask them to include examples and self-assess their effectiveness. For example, use a Likert scale from 1 to 7 accompanied with opportunities to make comments. Teach one of the teams how to do picture forming, emphasizing that they should consciously avoid suggesting solutions. (A facilitator can direct that any solution offered be put on a separate chart and redirecting attention to describing the situation.) At the end of the picture forming sessions, have the team members record their impressions of the utility of the process. One month later repeat the pre-measure as a post-measure by assessing again both teams' overall problem solving process. If the results are positive, repeat the experiment with more teams to validate the results and lay the groundwork for expanding the requirement to do picture forming to all teams (including the board).

Probe: How can we include customer feedback in each board meeting?

Background: We are aware of an international professional organization that promotes and supports their customers (practitioners of a special advisory process) with an elaborate website that helps the public find a nearby practitioner. The board decided to save money by cutting back on the website. The organization's manager tried to warn them not to do so. The results were just as the manager predicted, great customer dissatisfaction. More than half the customers left and the organization plunged into crisis.

Hypothesis: If a board checks its proposed decisions by asking, before each decision is finalized, "How will our customers be impacted by the decision?" the quality of its decisions will improve.

Experiment: Before formally adopting a proposal, the board meeting facilitator asks each person present, "How do you think our customers will perceive and be impacted by this proposed decision." If any board member expresses doubts about the positive impact for the customer, the facilitator guides decision improvement. At the end of the meeting, the facilitator leads an evaluation of the meeting by asking each participant, "How did the customer focus questions affect the quality of our decisions?" If the effect was positive, continue this technique in future meetings.

10.2 Understanding Your Customer

In Part II we uncovered:

- Ensure that the customer can learn from the deliveries and that the company can learn from the customer - both throughout the production process. (Constant customer focus)
- Observe and understand the end users' needs. Use the concept of personas for ensuring this understanding. (Constant customer focus)
- Build scenarios, or rather user stories to comprehend how the product or service will help solve the end users' problems. (Constant customer focus)
- Be sure to get early and frequent feedback from your customer in order to build the right thing, which means iterate, iterate, and iterate again. (Constant customer focus)

Probe: Can our customers learn from us and would that be attractive to them?

Background: The software industry has become expert in using Agile to build customer learning. Customers deepen their understanding of their own requirements by playing with interim software products as delivered at the end of sprints. They learn by coming up with different ideas about how the product could better support their process. They may even get insights about how to improve their process.

It is not so clear how to give customers this experience in other business domains, particularly traditional ones where there are established patterns, for example, restaurant or healthcare businesses. However, the authors are aware of some examples of innovation in classic businesses. For example:

- One restaurant asks its customers before taking their food order, "please say the name of someone for whom you feel gratitude." The learning that occurs is the deepening that comes from reflection. The restaurant patrons are likely to converse in a different way with the server and among each other and gain new insights into each other's values.

- An elder care facility gets food through a direct farm to table arrangement. It also transports the residents to the farm to observe the farm operations and even do certain parts of the farm work if they choose.

- A shoe company involves customers in the design process or rather lets the customers design their own shoes. The customers gain a deeper understanding of how they walk and their bodies' requirements.

- Some credit card institutions enable the customer to configure the date they will receive their credit card invoice. This empowerment means the customer can change the duration of their credit (within some limits). Some institutions also allow the customer to define the upper limit for the credit, which helps some customers not to spend more than they can afford and additionally reduces the risk of abuse in case of losing the card. The customers are encouraged to reflect on their own financial needs and spending habits in order to grow in self-responsibility.

For all these different scenarios, personas help the companies learn about their customers and come up with ideas for them.

Hypothesis: By giving customers the chance to interact with your business process, by introducing personas for them to self-identify, and by creating learning opportunities, the customer will be more engaged, loyal, and do repeat business.

Experiment: Reflect on your (potential) customers. Visit and talk with your customers or otherwise observe them to understand their struggles. Determine ways to involve your customers in your processes that would provide them learning. Or, come up with specific descriptions (personas) for some of the customers and create scenarios that would help resolve their struggles. Use a lean startup process to identify some minimum viable products you could introduce to these customers (see Ries). Construct an A/B test to see whether you and your customers are actually learning. Does that learning create a stronger bond between you and your customers around your products or services?

10.3 Production

We learned in Part II:

- Eliminate time wasted by deleting (or at least reducing) the activities and processes that are not focusing on the customer as uncovered by a value stream analysis. Thus, don't make the customer wait. (Constant customer focus)

Probe: Can you have a process that is "in flow?"

Background: Are wait times a significant challenge for your customers? Competition brings pressure to reduce wait times. Customers don't like to wait. There are whole professional areas (known as lean production or lean software development) focused on inventory management and operations research to streamline the product to customer or service to customer pipeline (see Liker and Poppendieck & Poppendieck). In your personal life you probably encounter frustrating waits in lines. In contrast, you also encounter situations where things go smoothly, like the primavera ballet dancer whose movements seem to be effortless. What makes the difference may not be obvious. Getting your processes into a state of easy flow takes the discipline of a dancer. (Like BOSSA nova dancers?) ;-)

Flow is not just about eliminating wait times. Sometimes you need lag time for getting into flow. Sometimes people try to reduce the wait time so much that things don't work. For example, the German train system tries to reduce the connection time between trains so much that it is too tight for some people to make the connection. The arriving train is a few minutes late or maybe you don't walk as fast between platforms as others. So, sometimes wait time is good for proper flow.

Hypothesis: You can treat production of products or service as a complicated problem where you sense - try to understand the problem, analyze - reflect on how you or others solved such a (similar) problem in the past, respond - use the (adapted) resolution from past learning and good practice. Operations research, for example, takes this approach. Yet experience indicates that achieving a flow condition is an art. If we assign a cross-functional team to focus on eliminating waste and optimizing process time as a way to optimize customer experience, we are more likely to get our systems into flow.

Experiment: Identify a customer interaction that is critical to optimize and form a cross-functional team to focus on it. The team should include customers, if possible, or a representative, and/or created personas reflecting your customers. Do a value stream analysis and look for particularly long wait times. Find a nuanced way to balance waste optimization and lag times that ends up "feeling right" to create an improved customer experience - neither tight and tense nor a slow burden. Use before and after measures of customer satisfaction to gauge the success of the process improvements. Note: don't forget that improvements in one part of the flow might not result in changing the overall flow. Empower the cross-functional team to do a value stream analysis examining the entire flow.

10.4 Feedback

No process, no feedback. No feedback, no learning. No learning, bumbling leadership. Every process should embed the possibility to get and provide feedback for personal and organizational growth.

Individual and Team Growth

To summarize Part II:

- During performance evaluation relate measurement to customer focus and organize learning and development for the individual so that it supports organizational growth. (Continuous learning)

Probe: Are performance evaluations really reflecting customer focus?

Background: Performance evaluations can become meaningless games, endured by staff and supervisors. They may include standardized corporate checklists that have little to do with the customers' actual needs. The team can work hard to develop outstanding skills and performance only to be told that the measuring must conform to a bell curve. So why try hard to develop? Or, there might be a measurement of "we will count the number of tests you write as a programmer and the more tests the better." Of course, a savvy programmer will then write lots and lots of meaningless tests. The authors are aware of a hospital that measures the productivity of its doctors by the number of surgeries performed! A customer-focused measure would be "number of patients made healthy."

Hypothesis: If customer focus is the foundation for performance evaluation, customer satisfaction improves.

Experiment: Choose a small number of working units, four for example. As a pre-measure identify customer satisfaction for each unit using your current method of determining customer satisfaction (surveys, interviews, repeat business, thumbs up ratings, etc.). Set up an A/B test: designate two of the units as controls and the other two units as experimental. Ask each of the experimental units to write their own performance evaluation criteria that is related to their work and reflects customer interests. Have the control groups revisit their current performance evaluation factors. After a defined timeframe, for example, a couple of months or many months, depending on the type of work, measure the customer satisfaction again using the pre-measurement methods. Did the customer satisfaction improve for the experimental units compared to the control units? If so, there would be several possible next steps. For example, have the control units start setting their own performance evaluation criteria and confirm that customer satisfaction then improves. Also, keep monitoring customer satisfaction for the experimental units to see if it continues to improve. You could also validate the experiment by repeating it with another set of units, and then consider changing the performance evaluation methods for the whole company.

Learning Strategies

We learned in Part II:

- Continuous learning follows a regular rhythm which creates space for feedback. (Continuous learning)
- Reflect and learn both from outcomes and from interactions. (Continuous learning)

Probe: Would creating a regular rhythm of team learning and reflection increase customer satisfaction?

Background: In software departments using Agile, it is a common practice to have regular retrospectives. In these retrospectives the team talks about what they have learned in the past two or three weeks from the results of the software they've delivered. They also learn from their interactions with each other, other parts of the company, and their customer. Based on the author's own observations, this practice has largely not been adopted by departments performing other kinds of work. In some occasions, the nature of the work may be "case work" focused (e.g. retail stores, doctors offices, or help desks) rather than project focused so that there is no rhythm with a clear beginning and ending. For this reason, it may be seem forced or artificial to introduce regular times for reflection and learning. It's easy to think of them as "we're wasting our time" or "something those egghead consultants make us do and we'll stop as soon as they leave."

Hypothesis: If we inject a regular pattern of reflection and learning into the work routines of units their performance will improve.

Experiment: Investigate to find a variety of work units in your organization that do not schedule regular times to reflect and learn. As in the previous experiment, do an A/B test, for example, three A units and three B units. Determine how to measure customer satisfaction for the units (find examples in the experiment above). For the A group, get their agreement to insert regular reflection and learning times into their schedule. Measure customer satisfaction at regular intervals for at least six months.

10.5 Innovation

In Part II we saw:

- The continuous learning process stays open to dramatically new paths that may emerge spontaneously by interrupting daily routines (e.g., moments of silence in a meeting, retrospectives especially when you are under stress, hold an ad hoc Open Space for new ideas). (Continuous learning)

Probe: Can we organize transformative learning?

Background: Continuous learning steadily accumulates new knowledge and skills over time. However, sometimes there is discontinuous learning, as you may have experienced when you get a sudden new insight that changes your basic framework and assumptions. Like the story about Newton inventing the theory of gravity after an apple dropped on his head, you suddenly gain the solution to a problem or, perhaps, compassion for someone you'd previously seen as an enemy. This discontinuous learning is often referred to as transformative learning. As we discussed in Continuous Learning, transformative learning may occur especially in times of chaos or rapid change.

However, a limitation of this view is that it casts you as a passive learner. You have to wait around for a crisis to happen before you can have a transformative learning experience. What if we could seek transformative learning as active learners? In the introduction of Part III of this book we encouraged you to use reflection. We've nudged you at the end of each Chapter in Part III. In essence, we've encouraged you to experiment with reflection as a method of learning.

Regular reflection is one method of being an active transformative learner. We suggest you also learn about other methods (see Kline). There is a lot of material on the internet. For example, we found Bregman 2009 and 2012.

Hypothesis: We can create a disciplined process for collective transformative learning.

Experiment: Identify a couple of units in your company. Using Open Space principles have them each separately spend a day in a conference Open Space format to focus in the morning on the question: "What are the basic assumptions underlying the way we are working?" In the afternoon they should focus on the question, "What if those assumptions were not true?" Ask the units to reflect at the end of the day and after three weeks about the value of the experience. Compare the results of the two groups. Did they both feel the experience was beneficial? Did they find similar benefits? Different benefits? Finally, assess whether the method produced results that were similar and reliable enough that you could feel confident in trying the approach with other business units.

10.6 Reflection

Follow the format of Adaptive Action from Human Systems Design in Chapter 6, Continuous Learning (see also Eoyang & Holladay):

Please take some time to recap *what* different probes were in this Chapter.

.... (these dots mean we're waiting for you to do that) ;-)

So, what are your insights about those probes? Again note them down.

.... (we're waiting)

Now what do you consider as your next steps given your context? Which one speaks most to your current situation? What are your plans for trying something like it?

.... (we're waiting)

11. Dance Around the Clock

"BOSSA nova" has many meanings, a new trend, a synthesis, and like a dance it always adapts to the situation at hand in non prescriptive ways. In any case, it is like a dance that keeps on going.

In this summary, we first look back at Chapter 1 and revisit the challenges companies face. Then, we suggest how you can use the probes yourself and encourage you to go beyond this book. The probes in this Part are meant to be a starting point and a source of inspiration for you to develop your own probes. We conclude with a glance at Agile Fluency Model and suggest a way to supplement it.

11.1 Revisiting the Challenges from Chapter 1

In Chapter 1 we identified the following challenges companies face: size, people, digital revolutions, VUCA, and collision of values. We also talked about the difficulties innovators have faced when trying to expand Agile to the whole company. In Chapter 2 we generalized the Agile Manifesto to four values and then in Part II we expanded on those four values by synthesizing four streams of development: Beyond Budgeting, Open Space, Sociocracy, and Agile. That synthesis was the basis for the probes we developed in Part III. We will now summarize how the probes help address the challenges that companies face.

Size

In Chapter 1 we mentioned the "elephant challenge" - how can a huge company be agile? Real elephants are actually quite agile. We even read a story about a friendship between a dog and an elephant. The dog would sometimes lie on its back and the elephant would use its huge foot tenderly to scratch the dog's belly (see Holland). As we've seen in Chapter 1, big companies typically have a hard time being Agile. Small is easier. Large companies might use Lean Startup or buy a company or have internal think tanks - all of these undertakings make parts of the company Agile but not the whole.

Probes that address the size challenge are mainly covered by strategy and structure. For example:

- Probe: Can we improve collaboration by changing the incentive system?
- Probe: Can our board of directors have the CEO and an elected representative on it without interfering with the work of the board?
- Probe: Is trust cheaper?

People

As discussed in Chapter 1, it is hard to find people who can deal with today's challenges. On the other hand, Millennials and younger generations are put off by the control processes typically used by traditional hierarchical organizations. These inhabitants of networks want to be able to follow their passions and expect equal access to information and equivalent voice in decision-making. In Chapter 7 we explored a new way of thinking about control of a company and suggested a new kind of organigram.

In Part III, we suggested a variety of probes for addressing people challenges such as:

- Probe: Will aligned individual growth happen without motivation by a bonus?

- Probe: How can we have autonomy as a team while supporting the organization's purpose?
- Probe: What would happen if we emphasized transparency company-wide?

VUCA World and Digital Revolution

Companies are constantly facing complex disruptions and rapidly changing market conditions. We suggest that experimentation growing out of regular reflection is a way to cope with these conditions. For example:

- Probe: Can we be more scientific?
- Probe: Can group reflection improve problem solving?
- Probe: Can we organize transformative learning?

Collision of Values

Should a company focus on the value of shares or on the value delivered to the customer? Boards of corporations are legally required to maximize value to the shareholders, which usually means *current* value of the shares. This valuation forces a focus on the short term. CEOs are measured by it. This short-term focus may often conflict with a longer term focus on value to the customer, and this conflict of values is one of the biggest factors that inhibit companies from coping with our rapidly changing world.

We suggest several probes to unscramble this conflict, including:

- Probe: Would it be worthwhile to establish mindful partnerships between production and support service teams?
- Probe: Should we change our legal structure?
- Probe: Is there an alternative to short-term profit focus?

Expanding Agile

In Chapter 1, in the section called Challenges With Expanding Agile, we noted that there are many commendable initiatives to expand Agile outside the software and IT departments. But there has been no holistic perspective on company-wide Agility that addresses what Agile means for companies' structure, strategy, or overall processes. Such a perspective would address organization structure and how departments are connected, the effects on leadership, and the meaning for shareholders. In addition, the overall perspective would address budgeting, legal, and personnel policies and reward systems. Finally, the perspective would explain what core Agile values like self-organization, transparency, constant customer focus, continuous learning, and even feedback mean for a company so that it can be completely Agile.

We believe that the synthesized values and new organigram we offered in Part II together with the probes we've discussed in Part III provide a practical, holistic Agile framework.

More work to do

The probes we list in Part III stake out a certain territory. We've addressed the challenges from Chapter 1, but what we've said is by no means complete. As we'll discuss next, we hope they will provide benchmarks that you can modify for use in your situation. We also hope you will explore far beyond them.

11.2 How to use the probes

You can start using at least some of the probes regardless of your role in your company. The effects of what you do will ripple out to your whole organization. Depending on your role, some of the probes may not apply to you, which is why we encourage you to reflect on what speaks to you - and let what emerges from your reflections guide the probes you try.

One suggestion is to start with one of the probes we've listed in Part III and adapt it to your own situation. Conduct the probe, analyze, and then change one parameter and try again. Meanwhile, publish your findings to your peers. This lean experimentation process will let you steer your learning.

Once you've gained some experience, try combining probes. Here's an example.

Example: Adapting the Hiring Process (Our own box)

Most companies have a standardized process for hiring people. Implementing BOSSA nova means having a more holistic view about such a process. We suggest a sample approach using different probes to create such a holistic view.

Start by looking at the *structure* of the hiring process with a *self-organized* cross-functional group from different parts and different hierarchy levels of the company. This approach will embrace different perspectives by using the probes: Is cross-functionality actually useful? and Would it be worthwhile to establish mindful partnerships between production and support service teams?

Then experiment with the *strategy* of making the hiring process *transparent* by probing What would happen if we emphasized transparency company-wide?. The goal of the strategy is to let everyone affected by a hiring process understand how and why particular decisions were made.

With the established cross-functional group *focus on the customer,* by clarifying who are their customers and seek for feedback from them about the hiring process. Are the customers only represented by the group receiving the new hire or are there other customers such as CxOs?

Reflect on how the hiring process can acknowledge these customers. Probe: Can reflective meetings improve customer relations? Then tryout looking from a *process* perspective by focusing on *continuous learning*. Run a retrospective with new hires (and the groups who've asked for the new hires) to learn from their experience. Use this feedback to adapt the hiring procedures. Probe: Can group reflection improve problem solving?.

And finally conduct an internal HR department retrospective focusing on the changes made for the hiring policies. Probe: Would creating a regular rhythm of team learning and reflection increase customer satisfaction?

Thus, by combining several probes we can experiment with the different perspectives of strategy, structure, and process. The result is a wider perspective, synthesizing different views, a common challenge we noted in the Introduction to this book.

11.3 Now Roll Your Own

In the introduction to Part III we suggested that you look at the probes we offer, compare them to your situation, and conduct experiments as visualized in the following figure from the introduction of Part III.

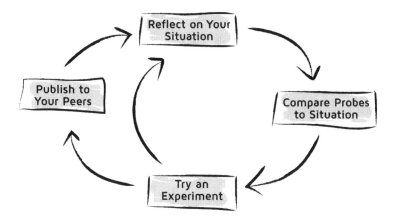

Keep Diving Deeper into BOSSA nova

We conclude Part III suggesting that you also go beyond the probes we offered and develop your own probes. Now the deep dive into BOSSA nova becomes an exploration of new territory.

We suggest the following approach to designing your own probes (and shown in the figure below):

1. Reflect about the situation of your company until an idea for a probe emerges. Decide if the probe should focus on your company's strategy, structure, or processes.
2. Design a probe: come up with background, hypothesis, and an experiment which includes some measurement.
3. Conduct the experiment. Analyze the results and loop back to step 1, above.
4. Publish to your peers along with ideas for new experiments. Based on peer feedback, loop back to step 1 and design new collaborative probes and implement new experiments - eg, widening the new policy to more parts of the company.

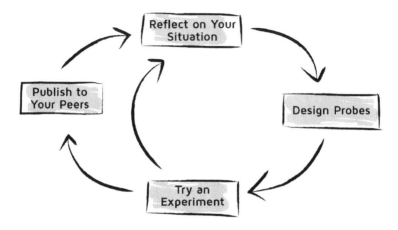

Explore new Territory with BOSSA nova

11.4 Systems Fluency

To implement the BOSSA nova in a way that holds up even under stress and achieve company-wide Agility, the whole company needs to optimize itself continuously.

There is already a model called the Agile Fluency Model that arose out of software but is applicable broadly. It describes how to become more fluent with Agile as a team and, therefore, also as an organization.

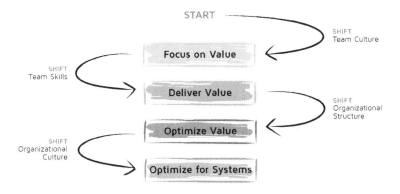

The Agile Fluency Model (version March, 2018)

We discovered in writing Part III that we could now suggest a supplement to this model. The founders of the Agile Fluency Project summarize the model in the following box.

Insights from Diana Larsen and James Shore, Agile Fluency Project

We co-founded the Agile Fluency Project with the goal that every team should work at the level of fluency that best fits their business' needs. The Agile Fluency Model describes an agile team's pathway. You can use the model to chart a course for the team, create alignment with management, and secure organizational support for improvement. Fluency is routine practice mastery that persists under stress. Anyone can follow a set of practices in a classroom setting. A team's true fluency level is revealed under pressure and in the face of distraction.

As the team adopts agile practices, a **team culture shift** occurs: instead of planning in terms of technical considerations, such as software layers or modules, the team now plans in terms of business, customer, or user benefit, exhibiting *Focus on Value* fluency. Mastery of technical practices like test driven development requires greater investment and, usually, more time. Once a **team skills shift** occurs that eliminates

technical limitations to delivering working software, the team
exhibits *Deliver Value* fluency. Where circumstances require,
the team may internalize the capability to understand and
address market needs. When an **organizational structure
shift** moves key business capabilities inside the team, the team
may exhibit *Optimize Value* fluency.

Agile development is fundamentally a team effort and the
success of an organization ultimately depends on its teams.
The Agile Fluency Model is a model of team fluency. Team
fluency depends on more than the capabilities of the individuals on the team. It also depends on management structures,
relationships, and organizational culture, as well as the tools,
technologies, and practices the teams use.

One-size Agile does not fit all! Once you use the Agile Fluency
Model to understand where your organization needs to be,
you are ready to start enjoying best-fit Agile.

Note that in this write-up Diana Larson and James Shore provided
detailed descriptions of three levels of fluency, leaving one level,
Optimize for Systems, open.

In concluding this Chapter we suggest a way to fill in the Optimize for Systems level. We suggest adding the following to their
description: "Mastery of a whole system perspective requires an
organizational culture shift with the team gaining an increased
understanding of, for example, cross-organizational value streams,
exhibiting *Optimize for Systems* fluency."

To help you judge whether your company is fluent in Optimize
for Systems, we offer seven indicators for self-assessment. To use
this assessment tool, ask every team member to reflect on each
statement and evaluate if it is true: Never, Rarely, Sometimes, Often,
or Always. Present the results and discuss with the team where you
all align as well as where you have the biggest differences. Develop

probes to explore those differences.

Indicators of Fluency in Optimize for Systems

1. The whole company identifies itself as a team. The language in the company is inclusive and does not differentiate between "us" and "them" (including shareholders and customers). That is, the team understands that its responsibility doesn't end with the team boundaries.

2. The team thinks of itself as a whole system that has a place and responsibility in societal systems.

3. The team stimulates the creation of new markets and invests in them.

4. The whole company develops through experiments - focused both internally and externally.

5. The team understands the value stream of the whole organization and contributes to its overall optimization.

6. Shareholder value, passion driven activities, and legal compliance align to create customer value.

7. The whole company uses intentional stillness or reflection time for making meaning.

IV Party Time

"No man is an island, Entire of itself, Every man is a piece of the continent, A part of the main." –John Donne

---

Thus far we've only had the perspective of a single company, but *no organization is an island.* We've mentioned relationships with stakeholders and customers but not looked at the complex web of society in which the company is embedded.

A BOSSA nova company has a responsibility to balance the interests of monetary profit, customer interests, inspiration of the work, and regulatory compliance. If the company doesn't live up to that responsibility, society will view it as untrustworthy. Customers, staff, regulators will see the company as untrustworthy. In the long run, that distrust will undermine the business.

For example, some years ago a large European insurance company announced that it would make a huge Agile transformation. Last year, it had a very profitable year, it was swimming in money - perhaps related to its decision to use Agile. However, the company has announced that it will sell its company sports facility, end the current employee subsidy, and rent it to a company that runs luxury fitness clubs. The company will make more profit from the property, but now many of the employees will not be able to have sports access. Society understood this news as "if the company is really Agile, why are they treating their employees like that?" and "that company is really greedy - watch out if they want to do business with you," and "I wonder what other damage they are doing?"

Your company is part of society. You can't avoid the party. How can you become a warmly welcomed guest?

The Four Values

For a BOSSA nova company the four defined values have both an internal and external aspect. The book concentrates mainly on the internal effect, because this is where it is implemented. Yet, the external effect of the values is as important:

- Self-organization: Regard the company as one node of a global network that creates the environment it lives in together with other companies and societal institutions.
- Transparency: Make the company's actions transparent both internally and externally. Today, there are more and more regulations in place that force companies to do exactly that (because it seems they didn't understand the importance of transparency and must be pushed by regulations). One example is the European regulation forcing the investment market to make all elements of a transaction transparent and traceable.
- Constant customer focus: Understand the economic, ecologic, societal, and social environment as a customer that needs permanent attention.
- Continuous learning: Learn continuously from and with society to make the whole world a better place.

Connected Perspective

The synthesis of perspectives shown in the following illustration from Chapter 7 shows only one outward connection - the customer.

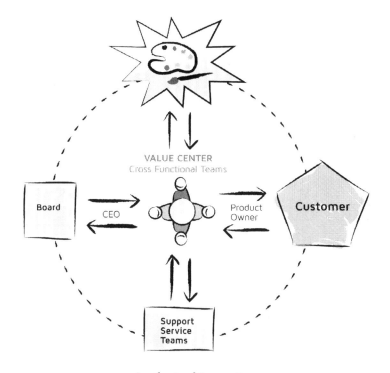

Synthesis of Perspectives

However, the other elements have to implement an external connection also, for example, the Board with the shareholders. The following diagram depicts these external connections. It looks beyond the "company island."

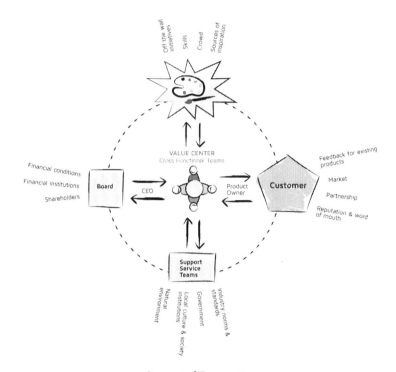

Connected Perspective

This connected perspective incorporates the surrounding environment (economic, ecologic, societal, and social) in which companies operate. They influence each other. Just as there can be an unbalanced relationship with the customer, the four values call for these other connections to be balanced, too.

The *Customers* emerge from the market. We've already talked about the direct feedback the value center receives from customers, but customers also give feedback to the market, for example, they provide Yelp[1] reviews as well as word of mouth comments. From the external feedback on existing projects, the company's reputation emerges. A good reputation prepares the market to embrace new products and helps to create a new market. It attracts customers

---
[1] https://www.yelp.com/

in a self-reinforcing cycle. Thinking back to Chapter 1, it creates a readiness to form partnerships for innovation that can lead to creative disruptions in the market.

The *Support Service Teams* interface with the "vessel of society" that makes it possible for the company to exist: the source of workers, legal constraints and protections, possible sources of support such as grants and economic incentives, the stewardship of natural sources the company uses, etc. These resources may sometimes seem stable: government regulations are about as hard to change as it is to move a mountain, the local culture has existed for hundreds of years, etc. Yet, even these "mountains" are actually part of the volatile, uncertain, complex, and ambiguous (VUCA) world. Governmental processes and the local society are often quietly controlled by a hidden trust network (see Chapter 7) and are quite capable of changing and adapting quickly - if they really want to. As a company, it is necessary to work with all environmental influences and not against them, which means respecting limitations and cooperatively leveraging them.

A traditional *Board* is an agent only of the shareholders and lenders. The Board members are often part of their own trust networks, and there are even laws against interlocking directorships that try to control the influence of such networks. For a company implementing BOSSA nova, the Board includes stakeholders other than the shareholders and ensures it is not constituted only by the so-called "good ole boy network." Beyond the Board, financial institutions that buy shares or lend money are subject to broad economic conditions, often volatile ones. Shareholders may be accustomed to a "culture of ownership" - shareholder as controller - rather than shareholder as participant.

The *Art and Spirits* are the passion and inspiration that bring creativity, joy, and commitment to work. They come from both inside and outside. For example, a company might go to the internet to ask its "crowd community" to design a new product or to come up with suggestions for improvements of an existing product, a kind of Open Space event with (unknown) customers, staff, and supporters. Or, the company staff may exchange new ideas with others who share their skills at meetups and user groups. The workings of inspiration may emerge in unpredictable ("off the wall") ways. We think of the group of programmers who decided to adopt a foster child or the development of Unix in the garage of two AT&T employees who were told "no" in their office. Sources of inspiration may include reflection, cross-field exchanges, and such values as beauty, equality, and ethics.

This connected perspective is another area that you may wish to probe as you develop your BOSSA nova practices.

Societal Awareness

As a part of the society, it is in the best interests of every company to "be a welcome member" of the society. There are different ways for ensuring this awareness. As inspiration we offer role model examples of companies that act from societal awareness for mutual benefit.

- Munich Re[2], one of the world's leading reinsurers, started to worry about climate change in the 70's. They started collecting and publishing research data about climate change early on. Protecting the research data for a competitive advantage is out of question for Munich Re because only transparency allows them to learn from others and to improve the data, which increases both the general societal awareness of climate change and their own resilience.
- The automotive company BMW tries to enforce fair labor in ore mines, an important source of raw materials. Ensuring good production conditions in the Congo is a good business

---

[2]https://en.wikipedia.org/wiki/Munich_Re

model according to Ferdinand Geckeler, sustainability manager at BMW[3] because the company's (or even industry's) reputation can be easily damaged by bad headlines.

- Buffer, a social media company understands transparency as one of their fundamental ethical values. For example, even their salary structure[4] is published. As a side effect of that transparency, they get more applicants and motivate people to use Buffer (see Zander).

- Telia Company made a decision[5] to divest subsidiary companies in several central Eurasian countries. It is a member of Businesses for Social Responsibility (BSR)[6], a network of more than 250 companies that aims to build a just and sustainable world. Telia sought BSR assistance in doing due diligence of potential buyers to minimize human rights risks, including the creation of a "responsible divestment plan."

- Microsoft supports rural communities[7] across the United States by transmitting broadband data over unused bandwidth. This lowers costs for broadband coverage by 80 percent and ensures that rural areas can catch up with the new economy. Microsoft has committed to bring broadband connectivity to 2 million people in rural America by 2022, which will improve people's lives through improved education, health care, agriculture, and business productivity. This project is supported by the Foundation Strategy Group[8].

In addition to these examples of single company initiatives, a BOSSA nova company can join networks that aim to improve the economic, ecologic, societal, and social environment, just as Telia

---

[3] http://www.sueddeutsche.de/wirtschaft/rohstoffe-sauber-bleiben-1.3809040

[4] https://open.buffer.com/transparent-salaries/

[5] https://www.bsr.org/en/our-insights/case-study-view/telia-company-human-rights-impact-assessments

[6] https://www.bsr.org/

[7] https://www.fsg.org/blog/how-microsoft-evolving-csr-efforts-help-rural-america

[8] https://www.fsg.org/

did. Following is a small sampling of such networks. What networks might be important for your company to connect to?

- Transparency International:[9] The global coalition against corruption gives voice to the victims and witnesses of corruption. They work together with governments, businesses and citizens to stop the abuse of power, bribery and secret deals.
- Global Compact:[10] A United Nations call for companies to align strategies and operations with human rights, labour, environment, and anti-corruption principles.
- Fair Labor Association:[11] An association that combines the efforts of business, civil society organizations, and colleges and universities to promote and protect workers' rights and to improve working conditions globally.
- Climate Group:[12] A powerful network of companies and governments to ensure prosperity by keeping global warming under 2°Celsius.
- World Water Council:[13] An international multi-stakeholder platform organization to make water a global priority. The Council focuses on the political dimensions of water security, adaptation and sustainability.
- United Nations' GAIN:[14] A global alliance for improving nutrition. It focuses on the health of employees through nutrition-sensitive policies. Companies benefit not only by a better reputation for taking good care of their employees but also by higher productivity. The network includes governments, NGOs, multilateral organizations, universities, and more than 600 companies in at least 30 countries. The

---

[9] http://www.transparency.org/
[10] http://www.unglobalcompact.org/
[11] http://www.fairlabor.org/
[12] http://www.theclimategroup.org/
[13] http://www.worldwatercouncil.org/
[14] https://www.gainhealth.org/

network has managed to reduce malnutrition by up to 30% in a number of countries. (see Hanleybrown et.al.)

- Institute for Multi Stakeholder Initiative Integrity:[15] A non-profit that promotes collaborations between businesses, civil society and other stakeholders that seek to address issues of mutual concern, including human rights and sustainability.
- Neighborhood Community Networks:[16] A bottom up structure to empower neighborhoods to organize into broad political and economic entities.

Besides being a way of connecting to societal issues pertaining to the company and a way of developing standards affecting the company, networks are emerging as a new form of societal and perhaps planetary form of governance. They are asking companies to serve a social purpose, harkening back in some sense to their original purpose when corporations first became popular as a legal form back in the early 1800s.

Insights from Tracy Kunkler, Circle Forward

"Society is demanding that companies, both public and private, serve a social purpose," writes Larry Fink, Chairman and CEO of BlackRock, in his January 2018 open letter to CEOs[a]. "To prosper over time, every company must not only deliver financial performance, but also show how it makes a positive contribution to society."

This opinion was confirmed in a recent survey[b] of a cross-section of Americans: 78% of respondents wanted companies to address important social justice issues; 87% will purchase a product because a company advocated for an issue they cared about; and 76% will refuse to purchase a company's products or services upon learning it supported an issue contrary to

---

[15] http://www.msi-integrity.org/introducing-the-msi-database-an-overview-of-the-global-landscape-of-standard-setting-multi-stakeholder-initiatives/

[16] http://neighborhoodparliament.org

their beliefs.

This survey reflects more than mere preferences. Our communities face life-threatening challenges in healthcare, poverty, food security, and climate resilience, as well as long standing racial, gender, and socio-economic injustices. To address these complex issues, more people are recognizing the basic interdependence that has been at the core of the field of ecology. As David Korten describes it, "life can only survive and thrive in community."[c] So, when Fink advises that "companies must benefit all of their stakeholders, including shareholders, employees, customers, and the communities in which they operate," he is acknowledging that more and more people are waking up to the deadly side effects of a single-minded focus on profit.

And, while markets will drive some degree of change, the picture is actually more complex. "No single entity, (or sector) no matter how large or powerful, can solve the complex problems in our current systems. Rather, the key to our success lies in optimizing the activities, relationships, and interactions among all the parts of the system."[d]

For complex issues, some of the most promising strategies are found when when all sectors – business, government, and civil society – come together to align their efforts for social change in **multi-stakeholder initiatives (MSI)**. This emerging form of collaborative governance[e] seeks to bring all the stakeholders in a system together – including those who have been traditionally marginalized – to participate in the dialogue, decision making, and implementation of solutions to common problems or goals. They are complex systems where authority, knowledge, and resources are interconnected and distributed across a large number of actors; therefore, power relationships cannot be organized hierarchically, but instead are peer-to-peer. There are a number of MSI examples in this chapter.

Such governance networks host opportunities for people to connect in-person and on digital platforms, and often take the form of distributed networks. In this way, any part of the network can be connected to any other part, at any time, without an intermediary, hub, or representative[f]. The decision to cluster around an emergent issue does not have to be vetted or coordinated by a centralized or decentralized hub, rather action can emanate from any point within the network. Therefore, government is often a key member of the network, but not necessarily directing the engagements. There is structural freedom to communicate, coordinate, and cluster around emergent issues; to assemble and disassemble as needed; and to bring together novel combinations of talent and resources to adapt to opportunities and challenges in the environment[g].

Multi-stakeholder partnerships between the United Nations, business, NGOs, governments, and other actors are playing an important role in the United Nations Sustainable Development Goals (SDGs). For global companies, the implementation of the SDG agenda offers transformative new business opportunities.

It is by participating in collaborative governance networks that companies have fresh opportunities to align their interests with society's rapidly changing needs and produce innovative solutions that generate new markets. "Collaboration between different actors with relevant knowledge, experiences and resources can create new ways of understanding a policy problem, develop new creative ideas, qualify the selection of ideas, transform and test the selected innovative ideas, evaluate their functionality, and finally diffuse them to relevant audiences."[h]

---

[a]https://www.blackrock.com/corporate/en-no/investor-relations/larry-fink-ceo-letter

[b]Cone Communications CSR Study, 2017. http://www.conecomm.com/research-blog/2017-csr-study

[c]Korten, David, "The New Economy: A Living Earth Systems Model" https://thenextsystem.org/the-new-economy-a-living-earth-system-model

[d]Gopal, Srik; Clarke, Tiffany, FSG, 2015. "System Mapping: A Guide to Developing Actor Maps"

[e]The term "collaborative governance" refers to a relatively

new and emerging field; this link is to some of the most widely used definitions from academics, practitioners and participants: http://tinyurl.com/CollaborativeGovernance

[f]Appalachian Foodshed Project, 2016. "A Regional Report on Community Food Security."

[g]Network Impact and the Center for Evaluation Innovation, 2014.

[h]Eva Sørensen, The metagovernance of public innovation in governance networks. Paper to be presented at the Policy & Politics conference in Bristol, 16th – 17th of September 2014.

Summary

Strengthening the web of society is a way to meet your company's responsibility for its environment. You can create your own probes about this outward responsibility in the same way as you can experiment with company-internal strategies, structures and processes.

Leave your island to enjoy the party!

Bibliography

For Part I - Gathering the Band

Agile Fluency: http://www.agilefluency.org/model.php

AgileManifesto: http://agilemanifesto.org

AgileHRManifesto: http://agilehrmanifesto.org/

AgileMarketingManifesto: http://agilemarketingmanifesto.org/

Andreessen, M.: Why Software is eating the World. The Wall Street Journal. August 20, 2011. http://tinyurl.com/jymevjd (last accessed, February 17, 2017)

BBRT: Beyond Budgeting Round Table. http://bbrt.org

Beer, S. (1995): Diagnosing the System for Organizations. New York: Wiley.

Beta Codex: http://betacodex.org/de

Beyond Budgeting Principles: http://bbrt.org/the-beyond-budgeting-principles/

Bogsnes, B. (2016, ebook): Implementing Beyond Budgeting. Unlocking the Performance Potential. Hoboken, NJ: Wiley. Kindle ed.

Brown, J. (2005): The World Café: Shaping our Futures through Conversations That Matter. San Francisco, CA: Berrett-Koehler Publishers, Kindle ed.

Buck, J. & Villines, S. (2017): We the People. Consenting to a Deeper Democracy. Washington, D.C.: Sociocracy.info

Cadbury, Sir Adrian: Shareholders versus Customers. Economia. October 13, 2013. http://tinyurl.com/jrdjv64 (Last accessed February 6, 2017)

Charest, G. (2007): La Democratie Se Meurt! Vive la Sociocratie! Reggio Emilia, Italy: Esserci.

Circle Forward: http://www.circleforward.us/

Cooperrider, D.: Introduction to Appreciative Inquiry. AI Commons. http://tinyurl.com/y8dlgygk Last accessed July, 2017.

Cynefin. https://en.wikipedia.org/wiki/Cynefin

DAD: Disciplined Agile Delivery. http://www.disciplinedagiledelivery.com/

Deep Democracy, http://www.iapop.com/deep-democracy/

Denning, S.: What Is Agile? The Four Essential Elements. http://tinyurl.com/y7c4jgtg October 15, 2017. (Last accessed December, 2017)

Drago-Severson, E., Blue-DeStefano, J., Asghar, A. (2013): Learning for Leadership. Developmental Strategies for Building Capacity in Our Schools. Corwin Publishers.

Duhigg, C. What Google Learned From Its Quest to Build the Perfect Team. The New York Times Magazine. February 25, 2016. http://tinyurl.com/zruz7tm (last accessed, February 17, 2017)

Eckstein, J. (2004): Agile Software Development in the Large: Diving into the Deep. New York, NY: Dorset House Publishing.

Emery, F.E. & Trist E.L. (1973): Towards a Social Ecology: Contextual Appreciation of the Future in the Present by F. E. Emery. Springer.

Endenburg, G. (1998, 2nd ed.) Sociocracy: The organization of decision-making; "no objection" as the principle of sociocracy. Eburon

Enterprise Scrum: http://www.enterprisescrum.com/

Eoyang, G. and Holladay, R. (2013, ebook): Adaptive Action: Leveraging Uncertainty in Your Organization. Stanford, CA: Stanford University Press. Kindle ed.

Follett, M.P. (2013): Dynamic Administration: The Collected Papers of Mary Parker Follett. Martino Fine Books.

GitHub: https://en.wikipedia.org/wiki/GitHub

Guldner, J.: Unternehmensstruktur: Die Mär von flachen Hierarchien (engl.: Organization Structures: The fairy tale of flat hierarchies. Die Wirtschaftswoche. August 29, 2016.
http://tinyurl.com/j2dlnds (last accessed, February 6, 2017)

Hesman Saey, T.: Proteins that reprogram cells can turn back mice's aging clock. Science News, December 15, 2016.
http://tinyurl.com/z3c5k9k (last accessed, February 17, 2017)

Hope, J. & Fraser, R. (2003): Beyond Budgeting: How Managers Can Break Free from the Annual Performance Trap, Harvard Business Review Press.

Hope, J., Bunce, P., & Röösli, F. (2011): The Leader's Dilemma: How to Build an Empowered and Adaptive Organization Without Losing Control. San Francisco, CA: Jossey-Bass.

HSD: Human Systems Dynamics. http://www.hsdinstitute.org/

Industry Analyst Panel, Agile 2016: http://tinyurl.com/hzevhj3 (last accessed, February 17, 2017)

Jacobsen, I., Spence, I. & Seidewitz, E. (2016): Industrial-Scale Agile - From Craft to Engineering. Communications of the ACM. December 2016. P. 63-71.

Laloux, F. (2014): Reinventing Organizations. A Guide to Creating Organizations Inspired by the Next Stage of Human Consciousness. Brussels, Belgium: Nelson Parker.

Larman, C. & Vodde (2016) B. Large-Scale Scrum. More with LeSS. Reading, Mass.: Addison-Wesley.

LeSS: Large Scale Scrum. https://less.works/

McKinsey survey: http://tinyurl.com/yc36w9zv
(last accessed November, 2017)

ModernAgile: http://modernagile.org/

Nexus: Exoskeleton for Scaled Scrum. Also referred to as SPS -
Scaled Professional Scrum. https://www.scrum.org/Resources/The-
Nexus-Guide

OpenSpaceWorld: http://openspaceworld.org/

Owen, H. (2008, 3rd ed.): Open Space Technology. A User's Guide.
Berrett-Koehler Publishers.

Reijmer, A. & Strauch, B. (2016): Soziokratie. Das Ende der Streitge-
sellschaft. Wenen: Soziokratie Zentrum Österreich.

Responsive: http://responsive.org and Zander, R.P. (2017): Responsive: What It Takes To Create A Thriving Organization. Zander
Publishing.

Robertson, B. J. (2015): Holacracy. The New Management System for
a Rapidly Changing World. New York, NY. Henry Holt & Company.

Rosenberg, M.B. (2015, 3rd ed.): Nonviolent communication. A
Language of Life. PuddleDancer Press. Kindle ed.

SAFe: Scaled Agile Framework.
http://www.scaledagileframework.com/

ScaledPrinciples: ScALeD Agile Lean Development – The Principles. http://scaledprinciples.org/

Scharmer, C.O. (2009, ebook): Theory U: Learning from the Future as
It Emerges. San Francisco, CA: Berrett-Koehler Publishers, Kindle
ed.

Semco: The Semco Institute. https://semcostyle.org/

Senge, P. et.al. (2011, ebook): The Necessary Revolution: How Individuals and Organisations Are Working Together to Create a

Sustainable World. Clerkenwell, London, UK: Nicholas Brealey Publishing, Kindle ed. and online: https://www.solonline.org/

Sheridan, R. (2015): Joy, Inc.: How We Built a Workplace People Love. Portfolio.

Snowden, D. (2000): Cynefin: a sense of time and space, the social ecology of knowledge management. In: Despres, C., Chauvel, D. (eds.): Knowledge Horizons: The Present and the Promise of Knowledge Management. Butterworth-Heinemann, Oxford.

Sociocracy3.0: http://sociocracy30.org/

Valve: http://www.valvesoftware.com/jobs/, https://en.wikipedia.org/wiki/Valve_Corporation

VUCA: https://en.wikipedia.org/wiki/Volatility,_uncertainty,_complexity_and_ambiguity

Waugh, R.: Mark Zuckerberg invests in CAPTCHA-crushing AI which "thinks like a human". welivesecurity. March 25, 2014. http://tinyurl.com/jmne5qa (last accessed, February 17, 2017)

Whitehurst, J. (2015): The Open Organization: Igniting Passion and Performance. Harvard Business Review Press.

World Blu: http://www.worldblu.com/

For Part II - Improvising the Tune

Agile Fluency: http://martinfowler.com/articles/agileFluency.html; http://www.agilefluency.org

AgileLucero: http://agilelucero.com/

AgileManifesto: http://agilemanifesto.org

Andreessen, M.: Why Software is eating the World. The Wall Street Journal. August 20, 2011. http://tinyurl.com/jymevjd (last accessed, February 17, 2017)

Beer, S. (1995): Diagnosing the System for Organizations. New York: Wiley.

Beyond Budgeting Principles: http://bbrt.org/the-beyond-budgeting-principles/

Bogsnes, B. (2016, ebook): Implementing Beyond Budgeting. Unlocking the Performance Potential. Hoboken, NJ: Wiley. Kindle ed.

Bogsnes, B. (2017, LinkedIn article): Hitting the target but missing the point - myths about target setting.
Online: http://tinyurl.com/ybf2fcc4 (last accessed January, 2018)

Buck, J. & Villines, S. (2017): We the People. Consenting to a Deeper Democracy. Washington, D.C.: Sociocracy.info.

Cynefin. https://en.wikipedia.org/wiki/Cynefin

Drago-Severson, E., Blue-DeStefano, J., Asghar, A. (2013): Learning for Leadership. Developmental Strategies for Building Capacity in Our Schools. Corwin.

Emery, F.E. & Trist E.L. (1973): Towards a Social Ecology: Contextual Appreciation of the Future in the Present by F. E. Emery. Springer.

Eoyang, G. (2009): Coping with Chaos: Seven Simple Tools. Circle Pines, MN: Lagumo.

Eoyang, G. and Holladay, R. (2013, ebook): Adaptive Action: Leveraging Uncertainty in Your Organization. Stanford, CA: Stanford University Press. Kindle ed.

Garland, Jr., Theodore. "The Scientific Method as an Ongoing Process". U C Riverside. Archived from the original on 19 Aug 2016. http://idea.ucr.edu/documents/flash/scientific_method/story.htm

GoldCard: http://tinyurl.com/j6q7b8a

Hope, J., Bunce, P., & Röösli, F. (2011): The Leader's Dilemma: How to Build an Empowered and Adaptive Organization Without Losing Control. San Francisco, CA: Jossey-Bass

HSD: Human Systems Dynamics. http://www.hsdinstitute.org/

Herman, M. (2016): Inviting Leadership in Open Space. A Guide for Training and Practice.
http://tinyurl.com/n2z4sg4 (last accessed April 14, 2017)

Ismael, S., Malone, M.S. & van Geest, Y. (2014, Kindle ed.): Exponential Organizations. Why new Organizations are ten time better, faster, and cheaper than yours (and what to do about it). Diversion Publishing.

ISO9000: Quality Management. http://www.iso.org/iso/iso_9000

Kepferle, L. & Main, K. (1995): The University of Kentucky Center for Rural Health. In: Owen, H. (1995): Tales from Open Space. Abbott Publishing. Available online: http://tinyurl.com/kldsu4b (last accessed April 29, 2017)

Kerth, N. (2001): Project Retrospectives. A Handbook for Team Reviews. New York, NY: Dorset House Publishing.

Krippendorff, K. (1986): http://pespmc1.vub.ac.be/ASC/Kripp.html (last accessed May 17, 2017)

Leybourn, E. (2018): https://www.linkedin.com/pulse/dear-company-you-business-make-money-evan-leybourn/ (last accessed February, 2018)

Mamoli, S. & Mole, D. (2015): Creating Great Teams: How Self-Selection Lets People Excel. Pragmatic Bookshelf.

Owen, H. (2008, 3rd ed.): Open Space Technology. A User's Guide. Berrett-Koehler Publishers.

Patton, J. & Economy P. (2014, Kindle ed.): User Story Mapping: Discover the Whole Story, Build the Right Product. O'Reilly Media.

Pedagogical Patterns Editorial Board. (2012): Pedagogical Patterns: advice for Educators. Joseph Bergin Software Tools.

PrincipiaCybernetica: http://pespmc1.vub.ac.be/ASC/PRINCI_SELF-.html

Reinertsen, D. G. (2009, Kindle ed.): The Principles of Product Development Flow: Second Generation Lean Product Development. Celeritas Publishing.

Ries, E. (2011, Kindle ed.): The Lean Startup. How Today's Entrepreneurs Use Continuous Innovation to Create Radically Successful Businesses. Crown Publishing Group.

Romme, Georges. Quest for Professionalism. (2016) The Case of Management and Entrepreneurship. Oxford University Press.

Rothman, J. & Eckstein, J. (2014, Kindle ed.): Diving for Hidden Treasures: Uncovering the Cost of Delay in Your Project Portfolio. Practical Ink.

Satir V., Gomori M., Banmen J. & Gerber. J.S. (1991). The Satir model: family therapy and beyond. Palo Alto, CA: Science and Behavior Books.

Schneider, J. (2017) Understanding how Design Thinking, Lean and Agile Work Together http://tinyurl.com/ya6kx7j9 (Last accessed November, 2017)

Wölbling, A., Krämer, K. Buss, C.N., Dribbisch, K., LoBue, P. & Taherivand, A. (2012): Design Thinking: An Innovative Concept for Developing User-Centered Software, in Software for People. Mädche, Alexander (eds.), Berlin: Springer.

For Part III - Shall We Dance?

AgileAlliance Experience Reports: http://tinyurl.com/ydf7uu3d

Agile Fluency: http://www.agilefluency.org/model.php

Beer, S. (1995): Diagnosing the System for Organizations. New York: Wiley.

Bregman, P. (2009): How to Teach Yourself Restraint. Harvard Business Review online: https://hbr.org/2009/06/how-to-teach-yourself-restrain.html (Last accessed August, 2017)

Bregman, P. (2012): If You're Too Busy to Meditate, Read This. Harvard Business Review online:
https://hbr.org/2012/10/if-youre-too-busy-to-meditate.html (Last accessed August, 2017)

Carver, J. (1997, 2nd ed.): Boards That Make a Difference: A New Design for Leadership in Nonprofit and Public Organizations, San Francisco, CA: Jossey-Bass.

Cooperrider, D.: Introduction of Appreciative Inquiry. AI Commons. http://tinyurl.com/y8dlgygk (Last accessed July, 2017)

Dignan, A.: The OS Canvas. How to rebuild your organization from the ground up.
http://tinyurl.com/yavden66 (Last accessed January, 2018)

Eoyang, G. and Holladay, R. (2013, ebook): Adaptive Action: Leveraging Uncertainty in Your Organization. Stanford, CA: Stanford University Press. Kindle ed.

Fu Y. & Huang ZJ. (2010): Differential dynamics and activity-dependent regulation of alpha- and beta-neurexins at developing GABAergic synapses. In: Proceedings National Academy of Science U S A. 2010 Dec 28;107(52):22699-704. doi: 10.1073/pnas.1011233108. Epub 2010 Dec 13.

Gomez, P. & Zimmermann, T. (1999): Unternehmensorganisation: Profile, Dynamik, Methodik (Das St. Galler Management-Konzept), Frankfurt/Main. Campus.

Herzberg, F., Mausner, B., Snyderman, B. B. (1959): Motivation to Work. 2nd ed. New York: Wiley.

Holland, J. S. (2016): Unlikely Friendships DOGS. New York: Workman Publishing Co., Inc.

Hubbard, D.W. (2014): How to Measure Anything: Finding the Value of Intangibles in Business. 3rd ed. New York: Wiley.

Ismael, S., Malone, M.S. & van Geest, Y. (2014, Kindle ed.): Exponential Organizations. Why new Organizations are ten time better, faster, and cheaper than yours (and what to do about it). Diversion Publishing.

Kim, W.C. & Mauborgne, R. (2009): How Strategy Shapes Structure. In Harvard Business Review. http://tinyurl.com/j2bn2ak (last accessed February 20, 2017)

Kline, N. (2015): Time to Think: Listening to Ignite the Human Mind. Cassell.

Kurtz, C.F. & Snowden, D. (2003): *The new dynamics of strategy: Sense-making in a complex and complicated world* In: IBM Systems Journal, Vol.42, No.3, p.462-483. Available also online: http://alumni.media.mit.edu/~brooks/storybiz/kurtz.pdf (Last accessed on April 5, 2017)

Larsen, D. & Nies, A. (2016): Liftoff. Start and Sustain Successful Agile Teams. The Pragmatic Programmers.

Liker, J.K. (2004): The Toyota Way: 14 Management Principles from the World's Greatest Manufacturer. New York: McGraw-Hill.

Manns, M.L, & Rising, L. (2015): More Fearless Change: Strategies for Making Your Ideas Happen. Reading, Mass.: Addison Wesley.

Mulder, P. (2014): The Kepner-Tregoe method: http://tinyurl.com/ydh652rp

Poppendieck, M. & Poppendieck, T. (2003): Lean Software Development: An Agile Toolkit. Reading, Mass.: Addison-Wesley.

Resnik, David A. (2013): The Role of Reflection in Leader Identity Formation in Small- and Medium-Sized Organizations. Ph.D Dissertation, Cappella University, UMI # 3593145.

Ries, E. (2011, Kindle ed.): The Lean Startup. How Today's Entrepreneurs Use Continuous Innovation to Create Radically Successful Businesses. Crown Publishing Group.

Shen, L. & Hsee, C. (2017): Numerical Nudging: Using an Accelerating Score to Enhance Performance. Association for Psychological Science. http://tinyurl.com/yaqmm3sg

SWOT: http://tinyurl.com/ls2ye7d

Valve: http://www.valvesoftware.com/jobs/,
https://en.wikipedia.org/wiki/Valve_Corporation

VolkswagenAct: https://en.wikipedia.org/wiki/Volkswagen_Act

Merriam-Webster: http://merriam-webster.com/dictionary/pattern

For Part IV - Party Time

Hanleybrown, F., Kania, J. & Kramer, M. (2012): Channeling Change:
Making Collective Impact Work. Stanford Social Innovation Review
2012.

Zander, R.P. (2017): Responsive: What It Takes To Create A Thriving
Organization. Zander Publishing.

Appendix

Beyond Budgeting Principles

From Beyond Budgeting:[17]

1. Purpose - Engage and inspire people around bold and noble causes; **not** around short term financial targets
2. Values - Govern through shared values and sound judgement; **not** through detailed rules and regulations
3. Transparency - Make information open for self-regulation, innovation, learning and control; **don't** restrict it
4. Organisation - Cultivate a strong sense of belonging and organise around accountable teams; **avoid** hierarchical control and bureaucracy
5. Autonomy - Trust people with freedom to act; **don't** punish everyone if someone should abuse it
6. Customers - Connect everyone's work with customer needs; **avoid** conflicts of interest
7. Rhythm - Organise management processes dynamically around business rhythms and events; **not** around the calendar year only
8. Targets - Set directional, ambitious and relative goals; **avoid** fixed and cascaded targets
9. Plans and forecasts - Make planning and forecasting lean and unbiased processes; **not** rigid and political exercises
10. Resource allocation - Foster a cost conscious mind-set and make resources available as needed; **not** through detailed annual budget allocations

---

[17] https://bbrt.org/the-beyond-budgeting-principles/

11. Performance evaluation - Evaluate performance holistically and with peer feedback for learning and development; **not** based on measurements and not for rewards only

12. Rewards - Reward shared success against competition; **not** against fixed performance contracts

Open Space Principles

From Wikipedia on Open Space:[18]

1. *Whoever comes is the right people* ...reminds participants that they don't need the CEO and 100 people to get something done, you need people who care. And, absent the direction or control exerted in a traditional meeting, that's who shows up in the various breakout sessions of an Open Space meeting.

2. *Whenever it starts is the right time* ...reminds participants that "spirit and creativity do not run on the clock."

3. *Wherever it is, is the right place* ...reminds participants that space is opening everywhere all the time. Please be conscious and aware.

4. *Whatever happens is the only thing that could have, be prepared to be surprised!* ...reminds participants that once something has happened, it's done—and no amount of fretting, complaining or otherwise rehashing can change that. Move on. The second part reminds us that it is all good.

5. *When it's over, it's over (within this session)* ...reminds participants that we never know how long it will take to resolve an issue, once raised, but that whenever the issue or work or conversation is finished, move on to the next thing. Don't keep rehashing just because there's 30 minutes left in the session. Do the work, not the time.

---

[18] https://en.wikipedia.org/wiki/Open_Space_Technology

In addition to these five principles there is a law available, called the "Law of Two Feet": If at any time during our time together you find yourself in any situation where you are neither learning nor contributing, use your two feet, go someplace else.

Sociocracy Principles

From Sociocracy:[19]

1. **Consent**: The Principle of Consent dictates that each policy decision (in which we make or change the rules by which we play) is made by consent. Consent is not consensus — it does not mean that everyone agrees. It means that nobody is aware of a risk that we cannot afford to take. We know we have made a decision by consent when somebody (usually the facilitator) asks "Can you see any risks we cannot afford to take in adopting this proposal?" If each participant in the meeting indicates they do not see any risks we cannot afford to take, we have made a decision by consent to try out the experiment described in that proposal. If policies are the rules of the game, then operations are "playing the game." While we only make policy decisions by consent, we can make operational decisions however the rules tell us to. Most often, this means very clear delegation of budgets and decisions to specific roles and assigning people to those roles.

2. **Circles**: The Principle of Circles tells us that a sociocratic organization is made up of circles – semi-autonomous, self-organizing teams that each make their own membership decisions, decide on their own working methods, and manage their own budgets. Each circle defines its policy (and some policies which apply to other circles reporting to it) by consent, and uses other decision-making methods as appropriate to its operational work. The key to the Principle of

---

Circles is that each circle is organized around delivering a specific type of value to a specific client (inside or outside the organization). A circle for an orchard would include growers, truckers, sales people, and accountants — or at least the people managing sub-circles devoted to those areas of work. Each specific type of value is known as an aim.

3. **Feedback**: The Principle of Feedback requires us to use feedback processes everywhere in our work, and especially in the power structure of the organization. While most companies have a top-down organizational structure, with managers providing links from one level of the organization down to the one below, those "single links" are often choke points for key information that people on the front lines know and the "top management" do not. Sociocratic organizations use "double links" to connect each circle with the one above it. The operational leader role provides guidance and prioritization from the higher circle to one below it, especially during normal operations. The representative role provides feedback and guidance from the lower circle to the one it reports to. While the representatives may not have any operational responsibilities in the higher of their two circles, they (along with the operational leader) are full members of both circles for the purpose of any consent decision-making.

4. **Election**: The Principle of Election by Consent provides an important counter-balance. While we can delegate almost any decision to operational roles or processes, using a policy decision made with consent, the one sort of decision we cannot delegate is the election of an important role — particularly the representative. Representatives must be chosen by consent of the circle which they represent. This ensures that the organization is woven together by a web of consent, and that power flows in circles through the entire organization.

Agile Principles

From the Agile Manifesto:[20] We are uncovering better ways of developing software by doing it and helping others do it. Through this work we have come to value:

- Individuals and interactions over processes and tools
- Working software over comprehensive documentation
- Customer collaboration over contract negotiation
- Responding to change over following a plan

That is, while there is value in the items on the right, we value the items on the left more.

Again from the Agile Manifesto:[21] *We follow these principles:*

1. Our highest priority is to satisfy the customer through early and continuous delivery of valuable software.
2. Welcome changing requirements, even late in development. Agile processes harness change for the customer's competitive advantage.
3. Deliver working software frequently, from a couple of weeks to a couple of months, with a preference to the shorter timescale.
4. Business people and developers must work together daily throughout the project.
5. Build projects around motivated individuals. Give them the environment and support they need, and trust them to get the job done.
6. The most efficient and effective method of conveying information to and within a development team is face-to-face conversation.

---

[20] http://agilemanifesto.org
[21] http://agilemanifesto.org/principles.html

7. Working software is the primary measure of progress.

8. Agile processes promote sustainable development. The sponsors, developers, and users should be able to maintain a constant pace indefinitely.

9. Continuous attention to technical excellence and good design enhances agility.

10. Simplicity–the art of maximizing the amount of work not done–is essential.

11. The best architectures, requirements, and designs emerge from self-organizing teams.

12. At regular intervals, the team reflects on how to become more effective, then tunes and adjusts its behavior accordingly.

Index

B

C

D

E

H

I

J

K

L

U

V

W

Y

Z

About Jutta Eckstein

Twenty years of experience in coaching, consulting, training, and development. Main focus on agile processes, patterns, project management, adaptive organizations, and advanced object-oriented design.

Jutta Eckstein works as an independent coach, consultant, and trainer. She holds a M.A. Business Coaching & Change Management, a Dipl.Eng. Product-Engineering, and a B.A. in Education. Her know-how in agile processes is based on over fifteen years' experience in project and product development. She has helped many teams and organizations all over the world to make the transition to an agile approach. She has a unique experience in applying agile processes within medium-sized to large distributed mission-critical projects. This is also the topic of her books 'Agile Software Development in the Large', 'Agile Software Development with Distributed Teams', and 'Retrospectives for Organizational Change'. She is a member of the Agile Alliance and a member of the program committee of many different European and American conferences in the area of agile development, object-orientation and patterns. At the last election, Jutta has been designated for the Top 100 most important persons of the German IT.

Stay in touch with Jutta:

- @juttaeckstein
- Jutta on Linkedin[22]
- Jutta on Xing[23]
- Jutta's homepage[24]

---

[22]https://linkedin.com/in/juttaeckstein/
[23]http://xing.com/profile/Jutta_Eckstein
[24]http://jeckstein.com

About John Buck

John Buck is the coauthor of We the People: Consenting to a Deeper Democracy, about sociocracy, a sustainable system for organizing and running organizations. In one sense, sociocracy is democracy specially designed for use in organizations. He heads a division of The Sociocracy Group, an international training and consulting organization headquartered in the Netherlands. John has many training workshops and sociocracy implementation projects for a variety of organizations. John's research and development is ongoing. For example, he is working with Fujitsu's advanced software lab to develop Weaver, software that helps meetings go better – in-person, online, and asynchronous. John Buck has extensive management experience with government and corporations, including managing large information technology projects. John is the first person, not native to the Netherlands, to be certified in the sociocracy circle-organization method. A founding member of The Sociocracy

Consulting Group, a division of TSG, an international consulting firm headquartered in Rotterdam, Netherlands, he has introduced sociocracy to a wide range of businesses and organizations, assisting them in designing work and making group decisions effectively by "rewiring" their basic power structure.

Stay in touch with John:

- @johnabuck
- John on Linkedin[25]
- Center for Dynamic Community Governance on Facebook[26]
- Sociocracy Consulting Group on Facebook[27]
- http://thesociocracygroup.com[28]
- http://www.dynamic-governance.org/[29]

---

[25] https://linkedin.com/in/john-buck/

[26] https://facebook.com/CenterforDCG/

[27] https://facebook.com/The-Sociocracy-Consulting-Group-465155886838177

[28] http://thesociocracygroup.com

[29] http://www.dynamic-governance.org/

Other Books by the Authors

We the People

Consenting to a Deeper Democracy

By John Buck & Sharon Villines

The 2nd edition of *We The People: Consenting To A Deeper Democracy* by John Buck & Sharon Villines was released in September, 2017 in both print and digital editions.

"Sociocracy is an essential tool for the 21st Century that in essence is simultaneously simple, human and practical." Martin Grimshaw

Since publication of the first edition in 2007, *We the People* has become the standard reference on sociocratic principles and practices and its history and theoretical base. It is a comprehensive presentation of the history, principles, and theory of sociocracy. It also includes "how to" information, reprints of historical texts, guides to meeting processes, a glossary, and a bibliography and index. The second printing, with corrections, is now shipping.

The second edition has been substantially updated and expanded. It remains the definitive handbook for learning about sociocracy and the method of designing and organizing our organizations that makes the collaborative of the 21st century actually workable. Not only workable, it creates workplaces and associations that are more effective, efficient, and harmonious. Its values are equivalence, transparency, and accountability.

Sociocracy based on consent decision-making for policy decisions, which are made by teams and departments. Teams, called circles, are interlinked in a hierarchical structure that is designed to optimize communications, especially feedback. The coordinating or general management circle includes members of departmental teams and makes policy decisions by consent of all its members. This ensures that policies are fully communicated at all levels and will be implemented smoothly and efficiently.

"Our understanding of how the world works was fundamentally altered when the mechanical model of closed, linear systems was replaced with cybernetics and complexity theory. Sociocracy is a governance method that uses these new sciences to design organizations that are as powerful, self-organizing, and self-correcting as the natural world, including the honeybees." From the book cover.

Retrospectives for Organizational Change

An Agile Approach

By Jutta Eckstein

About the book:

In this book, Jutta Eckstein examines how retrospectives —originally a kind of a facilitated workshop for gaining feedback— can be applied conceptually to initiate and implement organizational change.

Technically, retrospectives were an instrument for a group to examine a past joint period of time and learn from that. The participants of a Retrospective for Organizational Change do not share a joint past, yet they learn from their different individual experiences and use this as a basis to form a shared future. The main strength is to leverage the experiences of a diverse group. Especially if the change is dynamic, which means the approach toward the goal is unclear or if it is complex, where the goal itself is in-determinate, Retrospectives for Organizational Change can provide a way to support the change.

This book covers the conceptual idea of using Retrospectives for Organizational Change and additionally reports on the feedback and experiences of its practical application.

Linda Rising says about this book:

"Of course, there are other books on the protocols and exercises for retrospectives, but these don't share the 'whys' of this important ritual. What Jutta has done for us is provide real experience reports that show how useful retrospectives can be and share her research around using retrospectives to lead change in an organization. Get this book and read it!" (Linda Rising, Co-Author of Fearless Change and More Fearless Change)

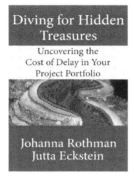

Diving for Hidden Treasures

Uncovering the Cost of Delay in Your Project Portfolio

By Johanna Rothman & Jutta Eckstein

About the book:

Does your organization value and rank projects based on estimation? Except for the shortest projects, estimation is often wrong. You don't realize the value you planned when you wanted. How can you finish projects in time to realize their potential value?

Instead of estimation, consider using cost of delay to evaluate and rank projects. Cost of delay accounts for ways projects get stuck: multitasking, other projects not releasing on time, work queuing behind experts, excessive attention to code cleanliness, and management indecision to name several.

Once you know about cost of delay, you can decide what to do about it. You can stop the multitasking. You can eliminate the need for experts. You can reduce the number of projects and features in progress. You can use cost of delay to rank projects and work in your organization. Learn to use cost of delay to make better decisions for your project, program, or project portfolio.

Have you ever wondered about how your projects become late? Are you worried that your projects become later and you don't know why?

Cost of delay can tell you where the delays occur and why. Common practices, such as multitasking, experts, and even other projects' delay can make your project late. Learn simple tools and methods for analyzing and eliminating the costs of delay in your project.

Agile Software Development with **Distributed Teams**

Staying Agile in a Global World

ʙy Jutta Eckstein

Agile Software Development with Distributed Teams

Staying Agile in a Global World

By Jutta Eckstein

About the book:

All software projects face the challenges of diverse distances – temporal, geographical, cultural, lingual, political, historical, and more. Many forms of distance even affect developers in the same room. The goal of this book is to reconcile two mainstays of modern agility: the close collaboration agility relies on, and project teams distributed across different cities, countries, and continents.

In *Agile Software Development with Distributed Teams,* Jutta Eckstein asserts that, in fact, agile methods and the constant communication they require are uniquely capable of solving the challenges of distributed projects. Agility is responsiveness to change -- in other words, agile practitioners maintain flexibility to accommodate changing circumstances and results. Iterative development serves the learning curve that global project teams must scale.

This book is *not* about how to outsource and forget your problems. Rather, Eckstein details how to carefully select development partners and integrate efforts and processes to form a better product than any single contributor could deliver on his or her own. The author de-emphasizes templates and charts and favors topical discussion and exploration. Practitioners share experiences in their own words in short stories throughout the book. Eckstein trains readers to be change agents, to creatively apply the concepts in this book to form a customized distributed project plan for success.

Topics include:

• The Productivity Myth
• Ensuring Conceptual Integrity
• Trust and Mutual Respect
• Virtual Retrospectives

Agile Software Development in the Large

Diving into the Deep

By Jutta Eckstein

About the book:

Agile or "lightweight" processes have revolutionized the software development industry. They're faster and more efficient than traditional software development processes.

They enable developers to embrace requirement changes during the project, to deliver working software in frequent iterations, and moreover to focus on the human factor in software development.

Unfortunately, most agile processes are designed for small or mid-sized software development projects—bad news for large teams that have to deal with rapid changes to requirements. That means all large teams!

With *Agile Software Development in the Large*, Jutta Eckstein—a leading speaker and consultant in the agile community—shows how to scale agile processes to teams of up to 200. The same techniques are also relevant to teams of as few as 10 developers, especially within large organizations.

Topics include:
- the agile value system as used in large teams
- the impact of a switch to agile processes
- the agile coordination of several sub-teams
- the way project size and team size influence the underlying architecture

Stop getting frustrated with inflexible processes that cripple your large projects! Use this book to harness the efficiency and adaptability of agile software development.

90037346R00146

Made in the USA
Columbia, SC
25 February 2018